PASTIMES
BECOME
PROFESSIONS...

VIDEO GAMES

Edited by Ben Van Buren

With Direction by River Accorsi

2019

THE V95 VIDEO GAMES SURVEY

The people speak. In May 2019, V95 disseminated a brief survey via their network. The survey was live for only 24 hours. The result was 321 responses—a snapshot, a biopsy of the V95 following, and their feel for video games.

Our guiding question, echoed most frequently in the pages that follow was, "What role will video games play in everyday life in 2069?"

CONTENTS

Introduction
Ben Van Buren,
Editor

This book is a crystallization, a screenshot of conversations about *what one can do* with video games today. Here you will find 9 interviews with individuals who make a living in some capacity by streaming games on Twitch, making gaming related videos on YouTube, commentating on live gaming competitions around the world, programing and developing original games, or hacking games to make art.

With two exceptions this book is a collection of interviews with people who use video games to create original video content (live or recorded) which is distributed on Twitch and/or YouTube. In many ways this book aims to be an extension of the social space that surrounds these plat-forms—a sort of slower chat scroll, or a long form comment section...

In conversations with content creators we focused both on the practical aspects of what constitutes this new profes-sion, as well as the emotional journey that goes along with deciding to make a career out of a favorite pastime. We wanted to know what their streaming rig looks like, as well as if they ever get lonely. Almost universally these creators are unified in the acknowledgment that they are inventing their career as they go, as well as in the assertion that what they are doing is absolutely a *career*, and not a fluke. These are serious professionals, building a platform and operat-ing within that platform all at once.

Bookending the 7 conversations with content creators are two interviews with people who work intimately with the underlying technology of gaming. The book opens with a conversation with John Romero, the co-founder of iD Software. John's work on Wolfenstein 3D, Doom, Quake and many, many more games is the stuff of legend. Here he opines on contemporary shooters and offers his thoughts on the future of gaming. Closing the book is a brief interview with the well known contemporary artist Rachel Rossin. Discussing Rachel's VR works invites us to meditate on the more philosophical implications of gaming and VR's ability to *immerse* the player in virtual experience.

The live social space that surrounds gaming on Twitch and YouTube can feel both intimate and distant. The chat and the comment section are slippery. They are quick. They can be warm and welcoming or toxic and abrasive. It's the hope of the editor that this book will offer the reader a chance to pause and contemplate these platforms and the kind of work and hanging out we do on them. *What does it mean to come together from so far apart? And how can we use a serious commitment to video games to both make and inhabit the world we share?*

Making this book has been a real labor of love and we hope you enjoy reading it as much as we enjoyed making it!

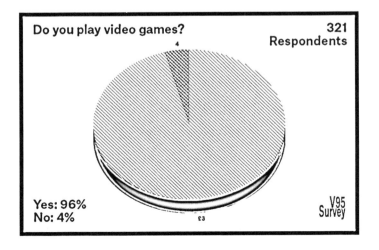

Do you play video games?   **321 Respondents**

Yes: 96%
No: 4%

V95 Survey

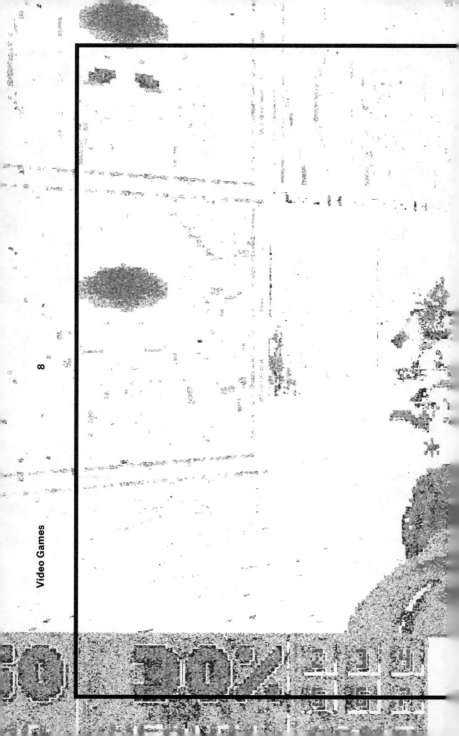

Video Games

John Romero

Designer, programmer, Developer

9

John Romero

*This conversation with
designer/programmer/developer*
John Romero
was recorded 3/08/19

V95   *Doom* is one of the most, if not *the* most influential shooters of all time. Given your experience with the genre I'm curious to hear your thoughts on Battle Royale games, which are currently very popular.

JR   After *Doom*, shooters branched off in a lot of different directions, which is awesome. I love the fact that shooters, and the design of shooters, have gone down so many different paths. From tactical shooters like *Ghost Recon* and *Rainbow Six* to competitive shooters like *Overwatch*, to *COD* and *Battlefield* and their entrenched styles of objective-based gameplay... It's a totally different rhythm. But the thing is, over the years, shooters have gotten *extremely* competitive. So if you're a new player you usually get killed really, really quickly. In *Call of Duty*, if you aren't really good, you're basically dead the moment you spawn. *Counter-Strike*? Forget it. You're dead before you even spawn. So it's really bad. [Laughter.] But Battle Royale gives people a feeling that they have a chance; because the map is so huge that you don't see another person for a while. And you get to control your spawn, which is really nice. Otherwise, it'd just be a basic deathmatch, which has existed since *Doom*. So you get gameplay before you get killed, and that, to a lot of people, makes it worth it. They feel like they have agency and that they have a chance. So Battle Royale has really captured a lot of more casual players that want to investigate shooters.

    Apex Legends is interesting right now. You wouldn't think that anyone should enter the Battle Royale fray after *Fortnite*, but the thing that *Apex* did really well was target the group that [*PUBG*] was going for. *PUBG* is not a kid's game, right? *PUBG* was for adults or teens. But it was just programmed in a very janky way. When *Fortnite* came in they captured the kids because the art style is very welcoming and really cool-looking. It's become the kid's Battle Royale. But the BR space was still waiting for an adult version to come and replace *PUBG*, because those two audiences—kids and adults—can co-exist. I think *Apex* captured the adults. Now, it's going to be harder for anyone else to get in. It's going to be interesting to see. I mean, I would never personally jump into the Battle Royale thing. But I think it's a totally viable genre, or sub-genre, and it's definitely going to spawn a lot more new evolutionary deathmatch styles from this point. It's changed the future of shooters. That geographical hugeness of the map is really important to people's happiness in the game. The satisfaction of being able to run around and maybe kill a person or shoot at somebody and live. [Laughter.] Plus people love picking stuff up. They're getting stuff, they're running, they're doing all this stuff and then they get killed. But at least they did some stuff... [Laughter.]

V95 Totally. At least you got to run around a little. I had also wanted to start by asking about something I saw on your website that I suspect will give us a sense of the breadth of your experience in the industry. What's the museum you're working on?

JR Let's see. We've been making games for 40 years, so we have a lot of stuff. And a lot of the stuff is not stuff that other people have. There are a lot of museums out there that have a Super Nintendo, an Atari 2600, and maybe some old game cartridges. Those are everywhere, and they're not interesting to me because I lived through all of it. I've seen it. I played them all. The stuff that's interesting to me is more like what's at the Strong Museum of Play, where I can see the hexagonal piece of paper that *Monopoly* was drawn on in pencil. I can see Sid Sackson's notes from when he was designing a game. To be able to see the artifacts of creation is, to me, way more interesting than seeing the final, finished product. Because [the artifacts] are what people can really learn from: how people went from A to B.

So, our archives have tons of stuff from the creation of first-person shooters, like all of the notes and drawings that were done before the *Doom* Bible was created in November of '92. All of the ideas: [ideas for] a good UAC logo, or a good *Doom* logo. Sketches and screen sketches of what things might really look like in *Doom*; and all of the notes—the handwritten notes—before anything was typed up. That's really cool. I've kept everything that I've ever made since I was a kid. From 1982 onwards, I have notebooks, I have tons of papers and printouts of source code, assembly language source code, BASIC source code. I have drawings I made, and advertisements I made for my games back then. I made dozens of games before getting to the point where I could create something new that no one had seen before. Anytime anyone hits a level of quality that defines something, you know, there are 10 years, 10,000 hours that came before that point.

With *Minecraft*, for example, Markus had written, I think, 28 or 38 games before that point. The original *Ultima* was game number 28 for Richard Garriott. *Wolfenstein* was game number 87 for me. We'd all published dozens of games people don't know about today. There were two shooters before *Wolfenstein* that were not very good. And we made seven platformers that redefined the PC as a game machine before that.

So: here's all of the stuff, here's the journey, here's all the bloody comics I used to draw as well... I have all of that too. But here's the concept art, sketches for weapons, concept drawings of maps... Just *all* the stuff. We've also got things from the early 1980s and '70s. Lots of cassette games from the very beginning years of the industry. (The industry started in '77.) There are a lot of cassettes from that period. And games from the 1980s. The Ziploc baggie games. I have at least 100, minimum 100 of those things, which are rare. I have hundreds. I have duplicates. I'm a collector. I have tons of stuff. This museum would have things that you wouldn't see anywhere else, which, in my eyes, makes it a more valuable museum. We have a building here and we have space on the second floor where all of our archives are, but we need a bigger space for [the museum] because we have so much stuff.

V95   When it's done I'll have to make a pilgrimage! You mentioned that it takes more than a few years, and a lot of different attempts to make a game of truly exceptional quality. Do you think that is something younger designers can appreciate?

JR   New people don't get it. It's a journey they have to go on. And at some point, maybe 20 years on, you realize you don't know anything. You know everything, but you really don't know anything because there's no ceiling. You can't know everything. But you know more than everybody else, right? So, you can start to help people to get there with you.

The young people are like, "Where's my Ferrari? I'm going to be famous," or, "I'm going to do something really cool." But the road is perilous. Most games fizzle out. They don't finish. It takes a lot of willpower to get a game done at a quality level. The people that persevere through that process are the ones who are going to be in the indus-

13

We Play Doom With John Romero

Meet John Romero: One of the Godfathers of the First-Person Shooter

John Romero On Commander Keen's Reboot, Doom Eternal, And Wolfenstein

In Conversation With John Romero - Doom, Wolfenstein, Commander Keen ...

John Romero

try and who are going to make it. Because they work hard.

V95   Helping people to make higher quality work through sharing what you know seems to have been fundamental to your philosophy as a designer and developer. Part of what made *Doom* so revolutionary, for example, was the how easy you made it for people to build their own levels. And as a result the modding community around the game is huge, and arguably has been an important training ground for many aspiring level designers. Why is it important to make games so easily moddable?

JR   Let's see. There wasn't really much modding going on before *Wolfenstein* happened, just because games were in assembly language, and the structure of the graphics and everything was just really cryptic back in the '80s. It's so much easier nowadays. With *Wolfenstein* it wasn't that easy, but people wanted to make levels for it so badly that they figured out how to crack it. And when I saw the unbelievable lengths people went to to make *Wolfenstein* run levels, John and I decided that the games we made needed to be completely open, that way people could easily modify them. That's why *Doom* was open. As soon as *Doom* came out we basically published the data structures within the map files and let people know how those data structures worked, so they could quickly write editors. We couldn't release the editor that we wrote, because it was on a different operating system, it wasn't DOS, it was on a NeXTSTEP. We just gave everyone the data and let them start making editors. And they did that immediately. There have been two million levels created at this point. We put out the BSP and the light programs that handled creating executable level files too. So we did the hard stuff.
    We did that because people want to be creative with that stuff—not everybody wants to create things from scratch. You don't create color from scratch, but you use color to make a painting. So we gave people a palette and let them create on their own canvas. And that's kind of what modding is: you give people the toolbox and let them

build with it. They're already having fun with the game; they love the game, they love the way it looks, the way it sounds, the story, and all that. They want to be part of the creation process as well. Modding is the perfect way to do that. Plus, if they're interested in getting into the industry; it's an excellent showcase of their skills for an interview.

We want other people to be successful as well. The only way for everyone to reach the stars is to have a lot of people aiming for them. The more people that have access to information and tools, the better. Being open helps create the level designers of the future. We're going to need them because, who's teaching level design? Sure, you go to a school and you learn level design, but maybe the person that's teaching isn't that good. I don't know: here's a game that's great, and here's how levels are made, and here's everything else. Just do it.

V95   Maybe this wasn't the intention, but being so open also seems like a pretty savvy business practice—a great way of keeping the game alive long after you are done with it. Was that intentional?

JR   Yeah. It runs counter to the way business people think because business people are all about locking it down. "Close it off, lock it down, sell them the thing, and then don't let them change it because we can sell them more of it later." Going beyond modding—for us, it was also important to give away the source code for the game, which is everything. There's nothing hidden anymore; it's like, "Here's all the code, here's all the data, you can modify it, you can change the executable, you can make a different game if you want to; you just can't sell it, but you can see how we wrote it." That really is the biggest reason why *Doom* is still alive today, because we released the source code and people made several source ports, which are amazing. That's how everyone runs it now. No one uses the original *Doom* anymore.

V95   Right. It has always struck me that the sources of inspiration for *Doom* are so fantastical. The common non-gamer might think of FPSs as being only set in 'realistic' environments and as using only 'real' guns, but *Doom* is set in space and there are demons! What were some of the inspirations that led to doom?

JR   Well, first, when we came out with *Wolfenstein* as the prototype of the FPS, the term "FPS" hadn't been invented yet. After *Wolfenstein,* when games came out that had similarities they were called "*Wolfenstein* clones." Then when we came out with *Doom,* similar games were called "*Doom* clones." There wasn't a name for the kind of game *Doom* was. "3D" was too general a term, and "First Person Shooter" hasn't been a thing until quite recently. What set *Wolfenstein* apart was that, before *Wolfenstein*, we hadn't used real, military style weapons. We were using wizard's hands, shooting fireballs, or *Battlezone*-style guns. It was only when we put an actual weapon in there with actual weapon sounds that it *really* worked. That's why *Wolfenstein* was such a massive hit, because those were actual weapons.

And then, we decided to set *Doom* in the *near* future because we wanted to both have weapons people understood but also cool weapons that don't exist. And we loved the chainsaw and the shotgun in *Evil Dead II*, so we're like, "We have to put those in this game." But those are way more *near* future. Ultimately, we went with more combustible weapons versus laser or magnetic weapons. Which was fine for us, because we like explosions!

The movie *Aliens* was another big inspiration. Just because there was a super scary, super fast enemy. You knew it was there and you were terrified. In the *Alien* movies, this xenomorph is the most terrifying thing. We wanted to have some characters like that, but we also wanted to have characters that you could just kind of mow down. But we didn't want everything to be too easy, too simple.

And then the *Dungeons & Dragons* element. The idea of [the primary enemies of *Doom* being] demons comes from a *Dungeons & Dragons* campaign that we had played for years. That multi-year campaign came to an end when

demons flooded the entire world and destroyed everything. We tried to survive that, but we didn't. The whole
planet was overrun by millions of demons and they killed
everyone, and that was the end of the game. We stopped
playing *D&D* after that, but we thought, "What if we made a
game that showed that? Demons from hell flooding in and
destroying everything?" And because we were thinking of a
space, sci-fi-type thing, that seemed like the perfect com-
bination: [demons] are not something you would expect in
a sci-fi game, right? You expect to find aliens. That's what
you do. You go to outer space and you find aliens. But who
goes into space and finds hell? Nobody's done that before
in a game. So that seemed like a really cool, new idea.

V95 Before we wrap up, I'm curious to know if you
regularly watch much Twitch or (gaming centric) YouTube?

JR I don't really... I know some people who listen to
streaming as they work. But I can't really do that... I watch
people streaming different things now and then. I really like
summit1g because I think he's just a really nice person. And he
can be really funny. (I love when he plays *Sea of Thieves*.) Usually
I just watch different people randomly on YouTube or Twitch.

AT SOME POINT, MAYBE 20 YEARS ON, YOU REALIZE YOU DON'T KNOW ANYTHING. YOU KNOW EVERYTHING, BUT YOU REALLY DON'T KNOW ANYTHING BECAUSE THERE'S NO CEILING.

John Romero

V95   Mostly to check out specific games, or do you follow particular people because you like their style?

JR   Yeah, both. I mean, sometimes I'll check out a stream just because I want to know something about a game. Because I haven't played the game, and I might not even know who the streamer is. In that case I don't really care. I just want to see the game being played. But typically, I'm interested in watching someone show off a game with so many mods loaded in it that it's a totally different game. I watch things like that mainly on YouTube, obviously, like everybody.

V95   To get ready for these interviews I've been watching a lot of modded *Mario Bros 3* and some speedrunning. It's just *fun* stuff.

JR   Yeah! Speedrunners! The whole speedrunning world. I watch a lot of speedrun videos too.

V95   Yeah? I love that stuff. I love the extremely glitchy, hacky, sequence breaking... all of that.

JR   Yeah, there are some really cool speedruns of *Super Mario Brothers*—the original *Super Mario Brothers*—where they've created Tool-Assisted Speedruns where emulators can execute button presses on specific frames so that you can have the perfect, non-human, play-through. It's crazy. I think even last year they discovered another thing in *Super Mario* that cuts some seconds off of the fastest possible play-through.

V95   Right.

JR   And I started—as in, founded—speedrunning.

V95   ... Oh?

JR   Yeah. I was writing a part of the *Book of Sigil*, for

SIGIL. At the beginning of the book I write about how speedrunning was not a thing in the '80s. Instead it was, "How long can you play on a quarter? How long can you stay in a game without dying?" So, as I was writing I thought, "Wait a minute, I've got to check my facts and make sure that [speedrunning] didn't happen in the '80s." So I did some googling and found a book on the history of speedrunning, and it turns out I'm the one who started speedrunning because I put times in *Wolfenstein*. [Laughter.] Then in *Doom* it really took off because you can record your runs and prove your time. So I was like, "Oh, okay. That's cool."

V95   Your career has so many firsts... Any last thoughts?

JR   I don't know. Games... they permeate the culture so much. I guess I'm really glad to see how games have taken over everything, from the gamification of stores to the replacement of television with YouTube. I think gaming is a superior form of entertainment, rather than just something you sit back and watch. I love the fact that people are actually *doing* [their entertainment]. In the future, people will probably become more involved in some other way. I know modding is kind of a part of that. And it might go to the next level, in a way. Somebody might show us a way for people who don't want to learn complex stuff to approach modding, almost in a *Minecraft* way. Maybe modding can become that kind of meta interface on top of everything, and that gets people even more engaged in the games they like. When it comes to games people like... Games that let you create the story are the ones that people get really attached to, versus the single-player, "I just go through the story, and I finish the story, and then it's over." People love that, but it's not as replayable as a game where you are making the story. I just love the fact that games are pretty much *everything* now. [Laughter.]

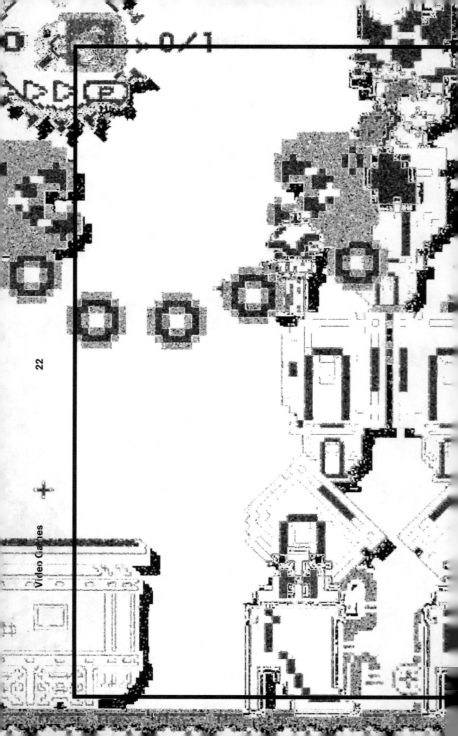

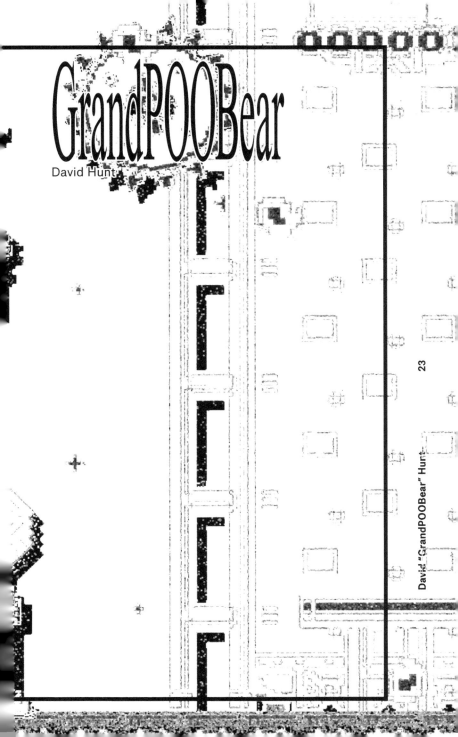

GrandPOOBear

David Hunt

David "GrandPOOBear" Hunt

V95   How do you describe what you do for a living?

GPB   Oh, I play video games.

V95   Gotcha.

GPB   I play video games really fast. That's what I do.

V95   Cool.

GPB   I play super hard *Mario* games that should only be beaten by computers, really fast.

V95   You truly do. You're on another plane.

GPB   ... Lots and lots and lots of hours.

V95   I've watched some speedrunning records on YouTube, but I know they mostly happen live on Twitch. What about Twitch lends itself to speedrunning?

GPB   Well, I mean, speedrunning is 100% on Twitch. Only highlights of speedruns happen on YouTube. The grinding, the practicing, everything else is really geared towards Twitch. You have chat interaction; you're doing the same thing, playing the same game over and over again, so the chat interaction definitely helps from time to time. Also there's nothing like being in a room live as a world record is happening. It's incredible, it's thrilling, it's exciting. There are also times when you get heartbreak, where a world record's about to happen and then there's a big choke at the end or something, and those moments can't be recreated on YouTube, pretty much. You set a world record on YouTube, you're labeling your video "world record"... What do I want to say? It's boring. "Spoiler alert." You know what I mean? That's like if you were watching the end of *Game of Thrones* and you already knew what was going to happen, you knew the White Walkers were going to win or something. Yeah. So doing it on Twitch adds a bit more excitement.

The other factor is that there's just a lot more money in Twitch, quite frankly. There's way more money in being on Twitch than there is on being YouTube right now. I heard a stat that Twitch only has about—was it thirty percent of the hours watched of gaming? But it's sixty-five percent of the revenue earned from gamers. So yeah... the way that system's set up right now, Twitch is a lot more profitable. And I think you're even seeing a lot of guys who have been on YouTube exclusively kind of realizing that—

V95   That's where the cash is.

GPB   —that's the future. Yeah.

V95   Sure, sure. Was there a specific moment when you realized that you wanted to start monetizing?

GPB   Originally I just started streaming because I needed something to do. I was a snowboarder before this and I was in a very bad accident. And the next year, I was going to have to sit out the entire year.

V95   Yeah? I'm sorry to hear that.

GPB   Yeah. Yeah. Well, I live in Lake Tahoe, which is snowboard town.

V95   Oh. Jesus. Yeah.

GPB   And once the winter rolled around, I was very lonely and very bored. I couldn't work, I couldn't go out and have fun with my friends, I just couldn't do anything. I had no purpose. And so my buddy showed me Twitch one day. He was like, "Hey, come watch me play *Halo*." And I was like, "Why the fuck would I want to watch you play *Halo*? Why would I want to do that?" But I turned on Twitch, and I did it anyway. Eight hours later, I was sucked into a rabbit hole of *Magic the Gathering* tournaments.

V95   Deeply hooked.

GPB   Yeah, just completely hooked, and a little bit later I was talking to my wife—I was like, "You're at work all day. This is what I'm going to do while you're at work all day." And so I just kind of started. And I definitely got into the whole vibe, the scene and everything... Originally I played mostly survival games, so besides speedrunning I really love survival games and BR games. That's my other favorite genre. But that's platforming... very different audiences, like, very, very, very different audiences.

Yeah, Battle Royale and survival games. So I love *DayZ* and *Rust*. And I played a ton of *H1Z1* back in the day. I love Fortnite. I haven't got to play *Apex* yet, but I have a feeling I'll love it as well.

V95   Yeah, it's pretty juicy.

GPB   Yeah, yeah, yeah... So I'm very into those games. Originally, I was kind of like an exclusive *Rust* and *DayZ* streamer.

V95   Okay. But you were already super good at *Mario* or not?

GPB   Well, yeah. My whole life I grew up playing *Mario*. My sister's ten years older than me and she got an NES when she was twelve, so my whole life I've always had an NES in my house and always had *Mario*. And *Mario 1, 2* and *3* were always the games I would go to as a kid...

So, fast forward a couple of years, maybe about a year-and-a-half after the injury and I was like, "I'm playing

I'M RESPONSIBLE FOR A LOT OF LIVES NOW, AND I DON'T TAKE THAT RESPONSIBILITY LIGHTLY BY ANY MEANS.

David "GrandPOOBear" Hunt

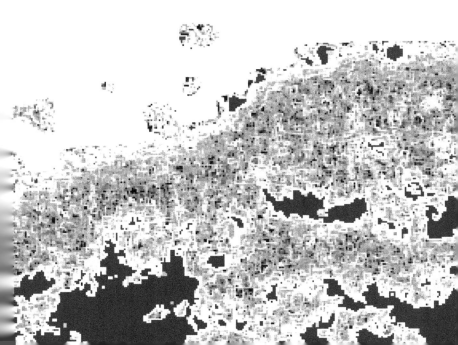

a bunch of different games and spending all this time, but I don't know how long I'm going to be able to stream this many hours, because you got to get a job and make money and support your family and all these things..." I was like, "Well, I really want to get good at one game before I have to go back to the real world." And so I picked my favorite game ever, *Mario 3*, and I started speedrunning it.

Originally, my goal was just to not be last in the leaderboard, and I achieved that pretty quickly, and then kept improving and improving. And then this game called *Mario Maker* came out and I was shown this guy named Panga—shown his levels—and I just really got addicted to everything this guy created: these really hard levels that also feature hidden blocks and other stuff to troll you. So it required not just incredible skill and platforming ability, but also memorization and recollection and repetition... And I just got addicted. Because you can see how many other people are beating these levels, and I realized quickly, "I'm one of only five people in the world that are beating these levels."

V95 Yeah, totally. You can see that clear rate and you get a little boost.

GPB Yeah. So the word started to spread around Twitch like, "Hey, there's this unknown who's beating these levels that these gods of gaming are also beating." And that propelled me from a 10- to 20-viewer streamer to 100- to 200-viewer streamer, and then eventually five, six, seven hundred, one thousand, two thousand... however many I get now, I don't know. So yeah, it's something that happened organically. It was never something I planned on doing. It was always something I just did for fun and then eventually I was making more money streaming than I was going to work, and getting off-stream to go to work was costing me money. Eventually, my wife and I sat down and decided even if I can only do this for a year or two years, I had to do it because not many people get an opportunity like that.

V95   That makes sense. So then, I won't ask you how much money you're making, but how many hours a week are you working? Could you regiment the schedule really seriously, or do you play it by ear? What's your feel for it?

GPB   I'm online for probably somewhere between thirty and fifty hours a week, depending on the week and the game that's out and how things are going. We just had a baby, so I'd say those hours are a little bit less right now than they usually have been.

V95   Congratulations!

GPB   Thank you so much. But yeah, that's [time spent] online. Offline there's another two to four hours a day, depending on the day, and then I run a podcast which is a big time commitment as well. I also own a company called Warp World, and we make tools for streamers, Twitch extensions, cue bots, just anything that we think is needed... Anything that's either not being made, or something we think we can make better, prettier, and easier, we make. Most of it we'll never make any money off of, but we do have some tools that are actually bringing really good revenue now too.

V95   Cool.

GPB   One's called Crowd Control, and it's a Twitch extension that basically allows viewers to pay money and alter a player's game live. So, like, if you're playing *Zelda*— let's say *Zelda: A Link to the Past*—you can summon a chicken attack, or take away all their hearts, or give them rupees, or kill the player outright, or warp them to the back of the dungeon.

V95   Who doesn't love trolling? And for five dollars you can too.

GPB   Exactly, exactly. Troll your favorite streamer for a

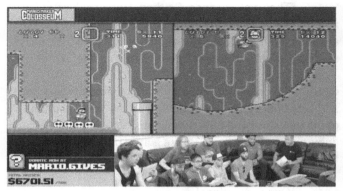

Poo And Ryu Vs Keys And Panga! Super Mario World Randomizer Co-op Race!

certain price. And that's been a very big popular thing for us, so we've been working really hard on that as well... It's an incredible amount of work, and then when you add in weeks when I'm traveling, it's just non-stop.

V95   Sure. Let's get into some details: what did you start streaming on, hardware-wise? And what are you working with now? And then maybe you could talk a bit more about Warp World and the kind of products you guys are filling the gaps with.

GPB   So, I mean, I started with just like... actually, my very first stream was on an Xbox app. That was my very first stream.

V95   Ah, sure sure.

GPB   And the Xbox 1 Twitch app, I think. I bought a pre-made Dell DC for like 600 bucks and that did me fine for a little bit, but you quickly want to upgrade as it goes on. I mean, now I'm working with a dual PC setup. I have every single console that's ever existed, ever. And that's not a joke. I have every single console of all time. Except for the Jaguar. I don't have a Jaguar or a Virtual Boy. Those are the two.

But yeah, that's what I'm working with now, and you just graduate. Now I have two PC's that are both worth more than my wife's wedding ring... And I have a nice DSL card camera set up, I have this really fancy system where I can control the camera angle, and pan and tilt and fade the camera anywhere I want.

V95   Oh yeah, I saw that on Instagram. It's got a little rig, right? You've kind of got a little film studio setup there.

GPB   Yeah, it is totally like a little studio setup. I actually went and did some hosting for a Twitcher at a professional studio and I saw what they were working with, and I was like, "Man, I got room for that at my house." So I splurged a bit... Got the most unnecessary piece of equipment ever, but I love it.

V95   Excellent.

GPB   Yes. So I went from starting on a console, and now I think my entire setup is probably ten or fifteen thousand dollars worth of equipment in here.

V95   Wow. And is that at your home, or are you in an office space?

GPB   I have my own room in my home... my office. We're buying a house and I'm going to build a legit studio in the house.

V95   What keeps you going when it becomes a job? I'm assuming there are days when you don't want to go to work, but you gotta go to work. Is it just the love of the game? How do you deal with that kind of job stress when this is something that you really grew up loving not as a career?

GPB   Well, that is hard. When your hobby becomes your job you have to almost find a new hobby.

V95   Have you found one?

GPB   I'm lucky in that I just love games. I love gaming. It doesn't feel like a job most days, but the gaming part—the playing of the video games—that's not the job. I'm going to use a bad parallel, but you always hear NFL players: "Oh, you pay me for the week. I do Sundays for free." Playing the games is the easy part. It's dealing with chat and assholes and the lack of privacy and things like that. And people asking the same question over and over and over again that you've answered 400 times. That's work.

V95   What kind of issues do you face in terms of not having privacy and dealing with assholes in the chat?

GPB   Well, a lot of it is people want to create rivalries. They don't like when streamers like each other. It's almost like pro-wrestling, it's really weird. They don't like it when they like each other. I'm in the *Mario* community, and we're all really good friends, but people want us to be super competitive and talk smack about each other. So they'll try and bait you into that, or remind you this guy is better than you even though you have a better time than him, or... I don't know. A lot of people just want to get a rise out of you. So that's hard.

V95   Do you feel like you have to be entertaining? Do you feel like you have to put on a show for them? Are you yourself on stream?

GPB   I would say I'm 90% myself. But if you're in a bad mood, you can't be in a bad mood on stream. Or if you are, you've got to be really, really funny about it. I definitely get in salty moods or cranky moods sometimes... I try not to do that. I try not to be a whiny brat or anything but sometimes— have you ever been to Dick's Last Resort, or those restaurants where the waiters are mean to you?

V95   I've been to one in Boston, I think...

GPB   Yeah, so every once in a while I have a day where I will just kind of just let it out, and that's one way to deal with it. The other way to deal with it is just to remember the fact that I'm living an incredible life. Sometimes it's hard and you don't want to deal with people, but all you can really do is put on a smile and answer the same questions and do what you can. It's not enough to just be on, live. You have to be *on* and happy and smiley and in a good mood, and your gameplay has got to be *on*. All those things apply. It's just part of your job, and it's just like any other job. I've had jobs I didn't want to go to before but I still went.

        I think the other thing is that I have a wife and son who rely on me. I have a video editor, and this is his full-time job. He has no other job. He edits videos for me— that's it. And if I fail, he fails, and that hurts his family as well. So I'm responsible for a lot of lives now, and I don't take that responsibility lightly by any means.

V95   And it seems that people really appreciate the work you do at your job. You've had two ROM hacks made in your honor. Who made them?

GPB   Barbarous King. And he's a full-time streamer, too. He's a huge streamer, he's one of the top thousand guys on Twitch.

V95   Wow. Yeah. How did it feel to have a ROM hack made in your honor?

GPB   Yeah. It's really crazy, honestly... A lot of ROM hack creators name their hacks after people they admire, that's kind of the tradition. And I've always said that nobody else can use my name except Barbarous King, because he's my favorite creator. And I never thought he actually would, but when he did do it, it meant a lot. What meant even more was just the tender love and care he put into it to include memes for me in the chat, or little inside jokes between me and him. This last one actually has a big giant puzzle at the end. It ends in this escape room. I love escape rooms. I love them. It's my favorite IRL activity to do; I love escape rooms, and this game ends in a giant escape room. It's awesome. But one of the coolest parts about it was one of the codes is actually—you have to get a cipher. I don't know if you're familiar with ciphers, but—

V95   Yeah. Yeah. Yeah. Yeah.

GPB   Yeah. Yeah. Well, the first part of the code for the cipher is my birthday, 4/11/85.

V95   Ahhh, nice!

GPB   Yeah. So it's just these little things—and I'm such a fan of Barb's, and for him to go out of his way to make me, specifically, an escape room... He knew everyone else would hate it, but that I would love it! [Laughter.] And not only that, but he included photos of me in the game, included memes and stuff in the game. It's just so above and beyond anything that's been done in the community, and above and beyond anything that I could have ever thought would ever happen for me. It's beyond humbling. You just can't top the feeling it gives you, it's just that warm, fuzzy feeling inside.

V95   Yeah. I mean, I can't imagine.

GPB   I love that.

V95   It seems like such a beautiful gesture. And when one thinks of a general video game community—in a very broad, kind of reductive sense—the average person wouldn't really think that there's work like that that goes on in the background. Do you think that's specific to the *Mario* and *Mario Maker* community?

GPB   No, I think every gaming community has tight-knit guys, and then there's some douchebags on the fringe. But if you look at the *Fortnite* guys—they're the most popular

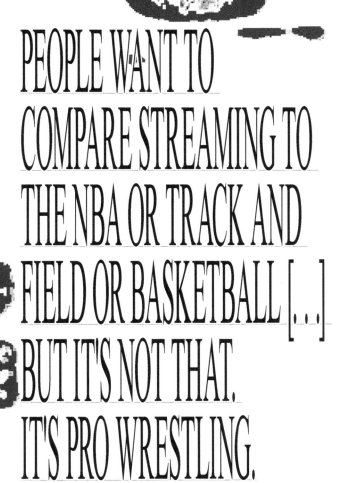

PEOPLE WANT TO COMPARE STREAMING TO THE NBA OR TRACK AND FIELD OR BASKETBALL […] BUT IT'S NOT THAT. IT'S PRO WRESTLING.

David "GrandPOOBear" Hunt

guys in the world. You have the nerd pack of Ninja and Lupo and TimTheTatman—they're their own little group of dudes. And then they have Cloak and Tfue beyond that, and FaZe Clan and the 100 Thieves crew, and they all collaborate with each other and play together. So you can see that there's genuine respect and love for a lot of different players and communities. I don't think it's exclusive to us. I do think because the way speedrunning is set up— speedrunning is definitely a more collaborative effort. It's competitive but it's also collaborative. Yeah, I want to hold the world record, but I can't hold the world record unless I get your strats.

V95   Yeah, the best strats can only be found because someone just beat your time, and you need to figure out how to beat them.

GPB   Exactly, yeah, so one person can't play a game and figure out every little speed strat; that's just impossible, it's not ever going to happen like that. It takes a village to optimize a game, and that's ultimately the goal. It's not just about me holding the world record, it's for the world record to be as low as it possibly could go. So I think that does lend itself to a bit more friendship and collaborativeness and creativeness between players. And the other thing is we get together.

V95   Yeah, that was my next question. Do you all hang out IRL?

GPB   My little crew of *Mario* players, we have our own event too. I guess I created it, but I consider it our whole community's event. It's called Mario Masters Colosseum, and it's where we just kind of all get together and literally do a four-day sleepover of just playing games.

V95   Cool.

GPB   Yeah. It's great.

V95   How else do you meet up? Are there specific yearly events you always attend?

GPB   Yeah, definitely Games Done Quick, Mario Masters Colosseum, and TwitchCon. We try to visit each other's houses if we can, especially if there's an event coming up like a race against each other or a co-op run with each other, stuff like that... We definitely try to get together, the *Mario* community. I'd say we're friends beyond just gaming at this point in the *Mario* community.

V95   So the community of gamers is strong, but what about the relationship with Nintendo? At one point they took down some of your levels (they got put back up later). And, ultimately, Nintendo could just decided to pull the plug on *Mario Maker* altogether. Does it ever worry you that Nintendo has that kind of power over the games you play for a living?

GPB   I mean, Nintendo's a very closed-off company compared to a lot of other gaming companies, especially indie companies. Speedrunners work with Indie companies a lot; indie companies love speedrunners, but Nintendo not so much, for whatever reason. I guess, yes, it's a concern... It's not really a concern. It's inevitable. I mean, all my levels got deleted, but then got put put back up and I ended up getting an apology from Nintendo, months later, after the whole news part of it died down... They contacted me and explained what had happened and apologized for the whole thing. I thought it was really nice. It was something they didn't have to do. It's not like I quit playing their games because of it. I still love *Mario Maker*.

V95   Totally.

GPB   I was quite hurt at the time, for obvious reasons.

V95   Of course.

Video Games

GrandPOObear   Videos 363   Clips   Events   Followers 156,903   ...   ⚙ Subscribe ▶

LIVE

⏱ 500

Breaking Ground on my last level

Category: Super Mario Maker • Team: Online Performer's Group

Modded   100%   Visual ASMR   Speedrun   English   Platformer

👤 1,290   ⊙ 6,154,065   ⬆ Share

GPB   I felt like I was losing my career, but in hindsight—I mean this is kind of weird, but it was probably the best thing that ever happened to me, because it got me a bunch of media coverage. And I know that sounds weird and horrible, but it was actually a kind of blessing in disguise. When it first happened, I thought it was going to ruin me; I thought people would think I was a cheater, or I'd get labeled a certain way, but it was the complete opposite. The community rallied around me. I got news coverage; generally, news outlets rallied around me; I got a lot of positive feedback, and I think it was also part of the catalyst for Nintendo to realize they need to be less closed off and more open and communicative with their fans. Because people eventually will just get pissed off. There are other games in town, you know?

V95   Sure, sure.

GPB   It was definitely an interesting moment. I mean... It's inevitable that everything in *Mario Maker* is going to disappear, that's inevitable. Nintendo won't keep the servers on forever. They're not going to transfer *Mario Maker 1* levels over to *Mario Maker 2*, or at least I don't think they will. And honestly, I hope they don't.

V95   Yeah, sure.

GPB   So it is—it's inevitable that it's all going to go away, but my memories of it won't go away and the videos of it won't go away, so it's not like it will be a complete loss by any means.

V95   Yeah, sure. Okay, yeah.

GPB   I mean, that's inevitable. *World of Warcraft*'s going to go away one day. I played a ton of *EverQuest* as a kid and my character is gone. That's how it is. Even saying that... My brother passed away when I was 19 and his character is gone. That's something that meant a lot to me. His character meant a lot to me. He loved *EverQuest* even more than I did and when he passed away, his guild—this is my favorite gaming memory ever—when he passed away, his guild put together this booklet and everyone in his guild wrote stories. And some of them were in-character stories. His character name was the Gatto. "Me and the Gatto were running through East Commons when we were approached by a traveler." It was like that. And then other ones were, "Brandon just helped me with this problem I was having while we were on a raid and he talked me through it." It's the best thing I ever got after my brother passed away, it meant so much to me. But his character's gone. Everything's gone. That's just how it is. If it lives in a digital world, it's going to shut down one day. If it lives in a digital world and it costs money to save, eventually it's going to shut down because, at the end of the day, gaming's a business. And, yeah, it means the world to me, but it's a business and I understand that it's inevitable. But I don't feel that takes away the memories or cheapens those moments by any means. They happened. I don't feel that means it's not worth putting in work for. I don't feel like that. No.

V95 That's a really beautiful story.

GPB Yeah, it's the best thing. It's the best.

V95 Streaming is a relatively new profession and you're one of its first new professionals. Given your experience so far, where do you expect streaming to be in five years? It seems to be growing. what do you think is on the horizon?

GPB Oh, man. I have no idea. I'll tell you right now it's already gone way beyond my wildest dreams—I'm a Red Bull Athlete now. When I was a snowboarder, there was nothing bigger than being sponsored by Red Bull, and now I'm sponsored by Red Bull for playing fucking video games. [Laughter.] It's really wild.

V95 Nuts!

GPB   Yeah. They sponsor me because I play *Mario Brothers* really fast. That's such a wild concept. I train with literal Olympians. Literal Olympic gold medalists, I go to Red Bull and I train with them. I do the same workouts they do. They treat me exactly the same—

V95   Wait a minute—

GPB   And all I do is play video games really fast.

V95   Back that up a little bit... You go to a complex, a place where they have space for you to train?

GPB   Yeah, they have two headquarters: one in LA and one in Austria. And, I mean, they treat all athletes the same. I get treated the same as Lindsey Vonn or Travis Pastrana or Travis Rice or John Jackson—

V95   Wow

GPB   —or any of their gold medal winners or their rock climbers or their divers or anyone else. I'm in the same gym, doing the same workouts. They have a whole eSports training program they're opening, as well. We'll have more focus on endurance and brain exercises, as well as the physical exercises. But, yeah. They treat me exactly the same.

V95   That's awesome!

GPB   Nobody there is like, "Oh, you're a *gamer*?" They're all like, "Oh, you're a gamer!" They're excited to work with gamers and tackle a new front. They're the greatest sponsor you could ever have for any sport, but especially gaming. They're incredible.

V95   Wow, that's amazing. I didn't realize that was something you did, honestly. I knew you were sponsored, I didn't realize that that was part of it.

What role will video games play in everyday life in 2069? *274 responses.*

Maybe there won't be line between video games, movies, or books. Just media that can be enjoyed by all.

as reflections of our dreams and memory.

no matter what year it is. People need an escape, an outlet and that is what video games will be used for the most, in my opinion. Video games will most likely keep a large playerbase among new generations as older generations digress, but will have grown into a more connected experience with users via the evolution of virtual reality and new steps in technology involv-

GPB   Oh, yeah... Calling it a sponsor isn't even fair. They're definitely a partnership. They want to support whatever you're doing. If you're doing cool stuff, they want to help you take it to another level, and that's what they do. They're great, they're amazing. I couldn't be more proud to be a Red Bull athlete, for sure.

V95   In five years, is this something you're going to be doing? In ten years? Do you have a sense of sort of your long-term plans for this work?

GPB   I don't like to think in five-year plans, because five and a half years ago, I was laying in a hospital bed and I thought everything that I loved was over. And now I make more money than I ever thought I could playing video games all day... [Laughter.] But I do think streaming is definitely—we haven't hit our peak yet. I don't think we're even close to hitting our peak yet. I think more and more brands are starting to recognize us, and as more big companies want to exploit us for cash that also legitimizes us to more and more people. In the same way that eight years ago not many people were streaming movies on Netflix—and now you literally don't buy Blu-Rays or DVDs because every-thing's on Netflix—I think we're going to see this transition away from... I'm trying to think of the right words. I don't want to say "traditional media," because that sounds so lame and boring. But as we become more mainstream, more and more people are going to give it a try, and as more people give it a try they're going to see that this is a form of entertainment that they enjoy—a form of entertainment that they want to dedicate hours and money to... So I don't think we're anywhere close to the peak. I always say, "I thought I peaked two years ago," and now just this week I'm having this huge growth spurt. So I don't know if I've peaked, or if I'm going to get bigger, or what—I can never predict that. But I definitely think that, for streaming as a whole, we haven't hit our top point yet. Our bubble has not burst. We're still blowing that bad boy up, for sure.

V95   What else are you doing to promote your brand as a streamer? Are you just getting online, and the word of mouth spreads? Are you promoting yourself other ways?

GPB   I mean, all of the social medias: the Instagrams, the Facebooks, the Twitters. You got to be on those. Instagram, I've noticed, is becoming a big driver. I think *Fortnite*'s huge on Instagram and that's spreading out to other games now. It's becoming a big driver for people to create content. So I think Instagram is probably the most important. Twitter is just like... that's gaming social media. Skateboarding's all Instagram, but Twitter is all gaming. So you've got to be on Twitter.

V95   I noticed that Twitter is kind of like the alert system for streaming. Like, I get all my notifications that someone is live via Twitter and whatnot.

GPB   Yeah, exactly. Twitter is definitely big for that. I also have a podcast that airs every Monday.

V95   What's it called?

GPB   We film it every Thursday and release it every Monday morning. It's called *The Warp World Podcast*. We talk about Twitch and Twitch culture, what's big on Twitch and what's happening. We give advice, take questions, just talk about whatever the hell we want to talk about, which is fun. That's another vehicle to get my stuff out there. I also really like that because there are things I wouldn't talk about on stream, opinions that you can't necessarily give with two thousand people about to respond to you, you know what I mean? We can get a little bit more political because art's political and games are art.

V95   Absolutely.

GPB   That's important. And I try to say yes to as many things as I possibly can. If there's a charity event that's happening, and I can help that charity event, I want to help that charity event. I want to help raise as much money as I can for good causes, so I go out of my way to help those charity events.

V95   Sure.

GPB   You always just have to be out there. There's always someone ready to take your place, willing to work harder, and better, and stronger than you. You've got to be better than that. I don't think it's a competition, I think there are enough viewers for everybody. I don't ever want to fall off my game. I want to go down as one of the best *Mario* players that's ever lived.

V95   Yeah. You really are an athlete. I can hear it in your voice.

GPB   I take it as seriously as I took snowboarding, so it's definitely something that I want to be great in...

V95   For sure. Any advice to someone who's maybe watching the Shaun White of *Mario* and wants to—

GPB   Wait, Shaun White, dude?! Okay, Shaun White is *not* the best snowboarder in the world and never has been. Travis Rice is the best snowboarder in the world [laughter] and always will be. Shaun White does competitions, and Travis Rice is a backcountry snowboarder. I'd much rather be called the Travis Rice or John Jackson...

V95   Ah! Understood... What's your advice? Someone who's ten years old right now, and who wants to have a stream like yours, and do the kind of work you're doing— what do you say to them?

GPB   Okay. The first thing is: you can't be just a gamer. Streaming isn't just about how good you are at video games. There are gamers that exist purely on their skill, that totally does happen, but the vast majority of Twitch streamers are big because of their personalities. So you need to have more going on besides video games. You have to have more life experiences to talk about besides video games, things that are interesting, so you need to go out there and live life. I don't think people get that advice nearly enough. You need to be open and have a life. It's wildly important. Everyone's like, "Work hard, be consistent," blah blah blah. Yeah, no shit... "If you're not on stream, obviously you're not growing your stream." Duh. But if you're on stream and you're boring as hell, you're also not growing your stream, and that's wasting more time. So you need to have more going on than just gaming, it needs to be more than just that. If you're ten years old, and I'm giving you advice: you need to go to college, man. You need to go out, meet people, kiss girls, kiss boys, whatever it is you want to do. Have experiences. Have some nights you can never forget and some you do. You need those times so you can call back to those funny moments on stream and tell those stories. That's important.

Some other advice you'll probably get from people is, "Be consistent." I hate that advice, just because it's obvious. My advice is: be well-rounded, but take yourself seriously. Take what you do seriously. If gameplay is important to you, treat it as important. You need to practice. You can't just get good at *Fortnite* by logging on and playing games every day. You need to go in and spend time practicing skills, practicing new moves, and coming up with things. You need to be constantly learning. You need to be researching what other people are doing. I call this R&D, "Research and Duplicate." How can you see what works on a stream, and how can you make it your own? And when I say duplicate, I don't mean just steal what they're doing to a T.

V95   No, no, no... It's like what you were saying about speedrunning competition. It takes a whole community to find the best strats.

GPB   Exactly, but own it. Figure out a way to own it. Figure out a way to make something your thing, your shtick. I think a lot of times people want to compare streaming to the NBA or track and field or basketball, where the best of the best rise to the top. But it's not that. It's pro wrestling. Streaming is pro wrestling. That's what it is. Being really great in the ring in pro wrestling will only get you so far. Being really great on the mic in wrestling only gets you so far. Being really great at both will only get you so far. You're then going to need a push from someone in power, you know what I mean?

V95   Yeah.

GPB   So you're going to need some luck in streaming,

especially with how many people there are now. There are three million streamers a month now—when I started, there were only three hundred thousand, and that was five years ago. That's an incredible growth! It's so hard to get noticed, you know what I mean?

V95   Yeah.

GPB   I think the last thing is: don't give up, and don't expect immediate results. My results didn't come for two and a half years. I streamed for two and a half years just for fun, it was just a hobby, it was just something I really enjoyed doing. I was playing games all day every day, and it was nice to have somebody to talk to. It didn't become a job until after that. If you're going in thinking, "This is going to be my new job," you're screwed already because you're just going to get depressed and sad and bummed out. So you can't do that. That would be my advice.

V95   Cool. Good advice. Thanks so much for taking the time to talk with us.

GPB   You're very welcome.

Hope it will be something close to a perfect for of escapism.

Completely in VR, you get immersed in an alternate world which kind of works like the one in Huxley's Brave New World novel, with the obvious exception of the Caste system. Everyone is truly equal, not because laws say it must be so but because everybody is bonded by the natural gamer-gamer relationship.

They could let you escape the limitations of reality, and the world would really be the way you want, because it's all virtual.

The whole point is, while that world will be "fake" in some way, it'll end up being more real than reality to to people who chose to live in it to a certain extent.

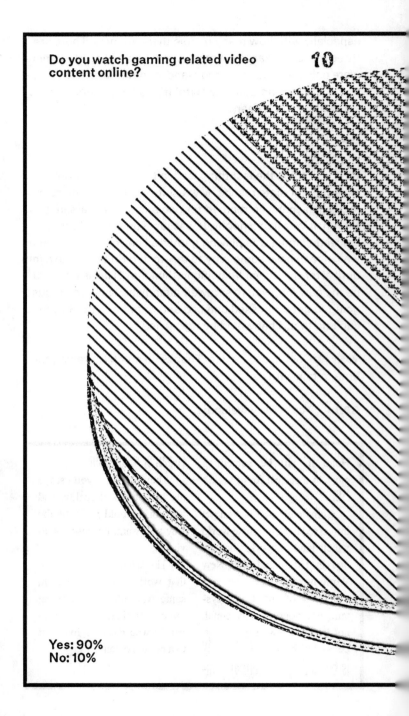

Do you watch gaming related video content online?

Yes: 90%
No: 10%

80

V95
Survey

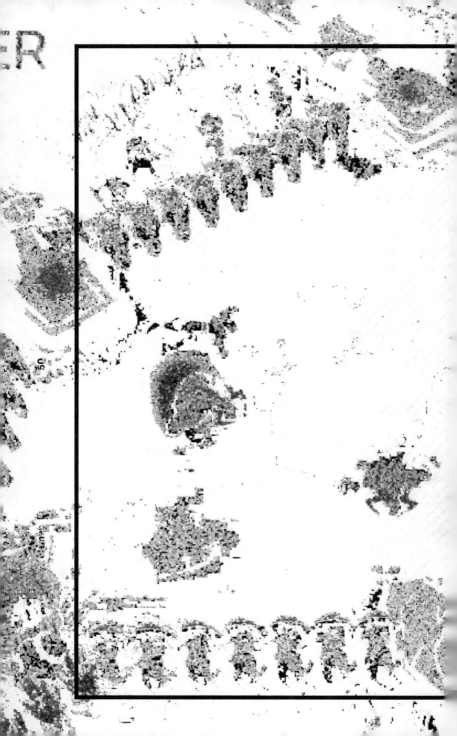

Sirithre

Gina Coleman

This conversation with
streamer
Gina "Sirithre" Coleman
was conducted via email during the Spring of 2019

V95   How did you discover Twitch and what was your experience of learning to use the platform?

S   I discovered Twitch back in 2013 due to a significant other being obsessed with *League of Legends*. This was also a time when I was struggling with a massive MMO addiction and was watching my shelf fill up with half finished single player games while I insisted on doing dailies and crafting in games that never technically end.

  Thus, my new year's resolution for 2014 was to quit playing MMOs, and to work on my backlog of games. So I started streaming in November 2013 to encourage me to stick to this plan. A way to have the multiplayer aspect of an MMO, while making progress on the many RPGs and action games that had piled up over the years. It was deceptively simple to get started. Throw a cobbled overlay together in photoshop, throw it in OBS and off you go. The real struggle was in learning the lingo and getting people to come back. Especially since I started out with semi-obscure PS2 RPGs. What was a Kappa? What did it mean to be raided? Why was it often hours into a stream before the first person managed to wander in? The regular struggles of a beginning streamer.

V95   How would you describe the evolution of your stream? What prompted the changes your stream has undergone over time?

S   At the end of 2014 I ended up attending PAX Prime in 2014 and despite being a nobody at the time, every single streamer I talked to was incredibly friendly, welcoming, and immediately absorbed me into their group.

From big streamers like DansGaming to small (at the time) streamers like AvalonStar. It wasn't until then that I truly felt a part of the community, but that was when I would keep streaming for years to come.

Over time we slowly built up an audience. A small group of people with the same love of the PS2 library trickled into my streams. Some of them started streaming too, and we'd stay active in each other's chat in an act of solidarity. We cultivated a following that would spread amongst our circle of friends naturally and without need for encouragement or promotion. We created a team later to be known as CasualRunsLive, a play on SpeedRunsLive for those who liked to just enjoy the story and play through at their own pace.

My second convention approached quickly—PAX South 2015. I wanted to do something personal for that small group of people I'd gotten to know over the last few months. So I offered to cross stitch their favorite emotes. I hadn't stitched in over a decade and I had an itch to scratch. A skill I could use to make something special for my friends.

None of us were partnered yet – it was a lot harder back then, and there was no such thing as affiliates; but we all had our favorites. I wanted to get permission from the emote's owner to use it, and thus offered to stitch them, one too. I mentioned my plans on stream one day and my small following convinced me to stream it, too. Creative didn't exist back then so I ended up broadcasting under no category, completely hidden from the Twitch directories, relying only on Twitter to get people in.

And it exploded. I'd tweet halfway in with a photo of my half-done project and a simple retweet from the emote's owner would manage to send a flood of people into my chat to ooh and ahhh and marvel over the novelty of someone playing with string on a gaming site. Some wanted to learn, others just wanted to watch and see if they could guess which emote I was working on that day as it came together. Others still just wanted a relaxing stream to fall asleep to without worrying about shouting and cursing and game mechanics.

I started making more and more and by the time PAX rolled around I had something like 30 emotes stitched and was averaging 75+ viewers a stream. It may not seem like much now, but it was more than I had ever expected and I was proud. And I've been stitching on stream ever since. Each convention I attended I'd bring 20+ emotes with me to hand out to streamers I looked up to. You can see those old projects here: http://sirithre.com/twitch-emotes/

I talked to Twitch staff later that year at another convention and not long after my partnership got approved.

Creative was born as a channel just a few months after that and I had found my niche and we reveled in it as a community. Things were going great.

Life happens, and I've had to stop and start multiple times. I took half a year break when I moved to California. I took another year off recently to write the official *Stardew Valley* cross stitch book. But no matter how long I'm gone the creative community welcomes me back in without question. The momentum is broken, but you learn who your core audience is. Those who come back regardless of how long it's been are those who you've really had an impact on. And that's an amazing feeling.

V95   You've mentioned in a previous email that you may be able to speak to the potential appeal of the Creative categories to non-gamers on Twitch. What has your experience of the Creative categories on Twitch been like? And, how would you recommend a non-gamer start their exploration of those categories?

S   From what I understand, Twitch can be quite scary for a non-gamer. There's a lot of lingo that only gamers truly 'get' and the learning curve is high. Creative is much more inclusive in that for most streams you don't need to understand games to explore. Sure a lot of the craft projects are game inspired, but they're still an art form that the average person can understand.

When the Creative category was whole and undivided it was quite easy to lure in crafters to this world of ours. But with it split into Art/Makers & Crafting/Music/ etc. it's much more difficult to explain where to even start looking. Now I have to guide people to https://www.twitch.tv/directory , tell them to ignore everything and to just type 'Creative' in the 'Search Tags' box. But then you run into the issue where a lot of creative streams go under IRL to get more views and makes it harder to find them mixed with all the chaos there.

As it is currently, it's quite difficult to explain to someone new.

The best we can do currently is lure new eyes into our own stream and help them explore with hosting and raiding. Creative channels are exceptionally friendly and welcoming for the most part, so it's a good first impression to our culture.

V95   What's your take on the overall ecosystem of Twitch? Are there any highlights you'd like to draw our attention to? Or, conversely, are there any negative bits that you feel need to be addressed?

S   As I mentioned above, discoverability could use some work. But I also don't know what *would* work. Twitch has grown so much it's hard to really keep track of just how many different channels there are let alone drive traffic to them.

It's a great place to learn though. Whether you're learning a new craft by watching someone else do it and being able to ask questions. Or by streaming yourself and having your viewers give you tips. Or watching a craft you're already familiar with and discovering new tricks you

might never have considered.

The same goes for the gaming side. From 'trying out' a game before you buy, being introduced to games you might not have discovered otherwise, or learning new ways to play your favorites.

V95 From an outside perspective the act of streaming can often appear to be both a communal and a solitary experience. Communal because one might interact with the chat and make friends with regular viewers; and solitary because one usually streams alone in a room. So, two questions follow: 1) Do you enjoy the communal dimension of steaming? Whether that's interacting with the chat, or finding ways to correspond with viewers outside of Twitch? 2) Does streaming ever get lonely?

S The reason I initially started streaming was a way to get the multiplayer experience of an MMO while playing singleplayer games. It's still my main reason for streaming. I work third shift, I don't leave the house much, and other than my significant other I don't get much social time. Streaming and/or the internet as a whole is my source of social interaction. And while that can seem lonely to an outsider, the connections I've made have been much stronger than any of my "real life" friends growing up. Whether just the catharsis of ranting about your day to someone, or the development of banter, inside jokes, and friendships as people start showing up regularly and learning your personality.

In the case of Creative there's no feeling like seeing someone try out a brand new craft because of you. Of being tagged on Twitter/Instagram when they post their very first project. Of seeing people truly excited to try out something that you love. Being thanked for introducing them to something they may never have even thought to try. That proud feeling of seeing their projects develop and seeing them grow in confidence as they create their first works.

Streaming is generally only lonely at first. No one knows to come to your stream. You're at the bottom of all the lists. If you haven't already made friends in someone else's stream chances are you'll be talking to yourself for a while. But it doesn't last long.

V95   What's the future of your stream look like to you? Are you actively working to grow the stream? Is this something you'd like to be doing in 5 years time?

S   I don't know where my stream will go. I'm not actively pushing for growth. I stream when I'm able, and if people show up, great! It's not a job for me, I'm not here for money. I'm here to make those lasting relationships with people who happen to have interests in common with me.

It certainly has led to a lot of unique opportunities for me. I got to beta test games like *Wanderlust Adventures*, *Interstellaria*, and *Stardew Valley*. I have met a number of developers and streamers alike in person thanks to kind viewers helping me raise money to attend conventions. I got to write and publish a licensed book of *Stardew Valley* cross stitch patterns to help get new people into my craft. I had a booth in artist alley at TwitchCon 2018, and have been featured on the front page and Twitch weekly multiple times.

In the end though, it's that handful of loyal friends who pop in to say hi any time I go live that keeps me coming back.

Esports will replace all sports in the olympic games

They will be taken more seriously as entertainment and art, due to the increased percent of people on Earth who play videogames by then.

I think they'll take up a chunk of everyday life; they already serve as an escape with it already being one of, if not the most interactive piece of media and with E-Sports on the rise, they'll only get bigger and bigger over time. The competitive scene will have grown exponentially.

I think video Games will bigger than to day. Everybody will play VR.

Games would be way more natural in public and it would evolve to a normal life activity for everyone.

the same as it ever was, as a hobby.

I think I will have kids by then and they will play them so i'll play the games with them

I feel that VR will be a basic console everybody has, and it will be a large part of our social interactions.

We'll have more grown men making careers off video games while jobs in the medical or science fields will be taken by robots. And once humanity is degraded to nothing but useless meatsacks, suicide rates will dramatically increase. As much as I love video games, i perceive them becoming less of a hobby and more the downfall of mankind. The professional competitions will only get bigger.

They will be intergrated into our everyday lives far nore so then they are today. Stuff like education and many other jobs. You'll be able to actually be in the game.

The same as it does now, to entertain. The entertainment will only get better, with the growing widespreading of things like virtual reality.

People will play video games not only as a hobby, but gaming jobs will become more and more important as we search for ways to entertain.

Gina "Sirithre" Coleman

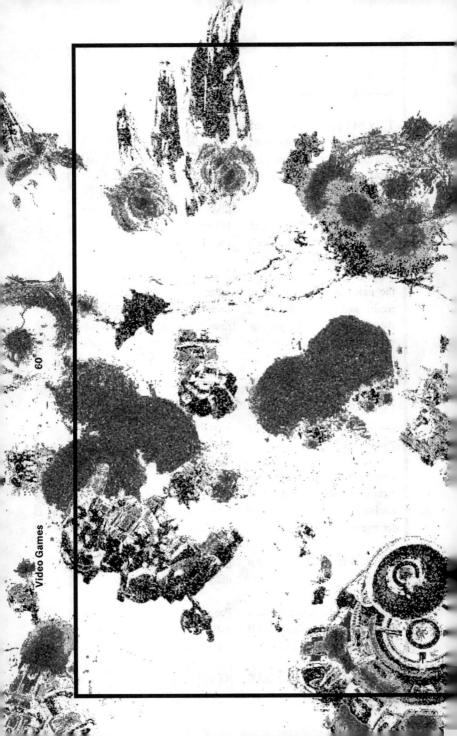

iNcontroLTV

Geoff Robinson

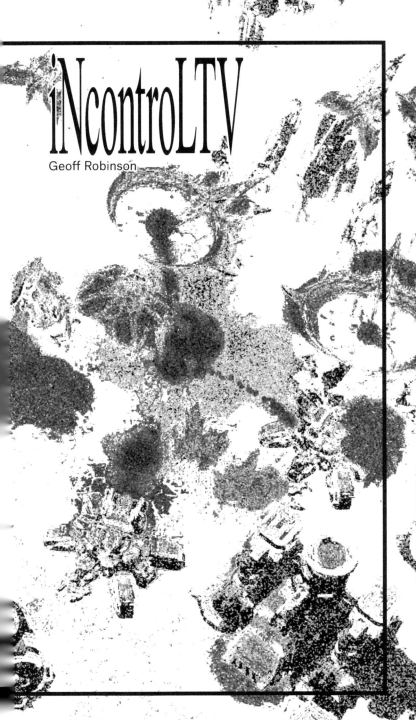

This conversation with commentator/streamer **Geoff "iNcontroLTV" Robinson** *was recorded 3/25/19*

V95   How do you describe what you do for a living?

ICT   Well, I think the nice thing about my career is that it's not an easy answer. I consider myself kind of an online gaming personality, but I guess you could even take out the "online" part, right? Because I do a lot of events and traveling. But I stream, I commentate, I kind of act as a hype man for some things, I do gigs, and then I get sponsored, and that's basically how I do my professional life.

V95   Are you mostly a caster, mostly a streamer, mostly a hype man?

ICT   I would say I'm mostly a streamer, but honestly, it gets pretty close to 50-50 with commentating, just based off of how busy I can be each year. I do just about every *StarCraft* event, and the ones that I don't do I often have a conflict with something else, or I say "no" to it as opposed to the opportunity not being there. It can be two or three—sometimes, in a very busy month, four—trips for commentating gigs, and then I stream in between that. So it's a lot of travel. It's a lot of gigs. It's very busy.

V95   Are you exhausted all the time?

ICT   It's funny, because each year I almost get to a breaking point. I'm like, "All right, well, next year I'm absolutely not going to do this." Truth be told, it is exhausting; travel just sucks. It's really fun when you don't do it a whole bunch, but when you do it a whole bunch, with everything that's happening, travel does kind of grind you down. But I really love what I do. Going to these events, seeing these people, being a commentator, being a entertainer... That kind of stuff is an absolute dream come true. So each year I'll be like, "I'm going to do less," and then each year I'm like, "Well, I'm not saying no to this one. Not saying no to that one," and there goes April.

V95   So let's talk a little about your commentating work. Give us a little of the back story.

ICT   Sure. So you're not going to hear me say that I looked at something, wanted it, and got it. It's more of a natural progression. I've been doing this for... Well, I've been playing *StarCraft* heavily since I was 13, but I became a professional at 18 or 19. And now I'm 33. So we're talking about 15 plus years of experience. I never really honed in on something and made it happen. What happened was that I won a national championship, so teams wanted to sponsor me and I became a professional player. And then, while being a professional player, my team—Evil Geniuses—was very media-focused, and I was one of the first people picked to do advertisements or speaking tours on behalf of Intel when they would come up. And from there DreamHack and other events were like, "How about you commentate?" and I just kind of naturally slid into it.

V95   And your most recent event as a commentator was IEM Katowice, correct?

ICT   Yeah.

V95   Bring us into the room. How close are you to the players when you're commentating on live matches? Maybe focusing specifically on Poland, what's the setup like there?

ICT   So for IEM we were in a studio, which is actually away from the players for the most part. We have an analyst desk. We have a caster station. For me, I was alongside people I've been working with for more than ten years,

63

Geoff "iNcontroLTV" Robinson

which is often the case, and we all have a huge passion for this game. I've been doing this for a very long time. One of the fun things about *StarCraft* is that, because it's been around so long, [the commentators] have been distilled down to our best people and our best events, which is really, really cool.

V95 So you're there. You've got your desk. Are you looking at just one monitor, or are there other things going on?

ICT Oh, tons of stuff, yeah. [We are usually sitting in front of a] preview screen, which is the direct feed of what's going on during the stream. And then we have two other screens which we can use to look up stats and basically have the internet at our fingertips. And then at the analyst desk, [where we talk about what's going on in between matches], you're standing. The analyst desk is a little bit more of a production. It's got some preview screens and telestrators. That desk has a host who's not necessarily the most knowledgeable about *StarCraft*, but who is fantastic at cohesively tying the show together and getting everyone feeling comfortable, that kind of thing.

V95 Right. The analysts desk looks a lot like more traditional sports commentating.

ICT Yeah, eSports has evolved. It used to be that commentators did everything, straight-up. But that can be very drab. So now we have a table host. We have analysts. The analyst desk is a way to break the monotony of two people talking at you for 12 hours out of the day. It also gives opportunities for more focused discussion and that kind of thing.

V95 Okay. So that's the day-to-day. And then, what's the scope of the entire event from when the wheels touch down when you arrive in Poland through to the last day? Are your days more or less the same in terms of the number of hours you're working?

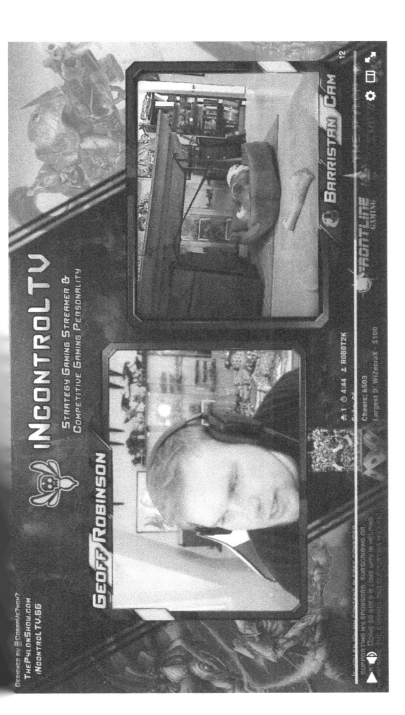

Geoff "iNcontroLTV" Robinson

ICT   They're generally the same. Getting into town, as a talent, is a lot about making sure to rest and get acclimated to the timezone. I'm on the West Coast of the United States, but [IEM Katowice] was in Poland, so it was a nine-hour difference for me. [The event] usually flys you there a day or two ahead of rehearsal, so you can sleep and rest for a day. It's a lot of money on the line. It's a very big production. So just landing and commentating is not something people do.

V95   Sure. What's rehearsal like?

ICT   Yeah, it's definitely more for the production than it is for us. It's about getting microphones adjusted and camera angles right and lighting correct and making sure that everything's working. But for us, it's nothing. The very honest answer, (pulling the curtain back), it's a lot of poopoo and peepee jokes and the laughing and being on your phone and basically wasting two to three, maybe four hours of our lives, but it's resting and it's fun and it helps you to get accommodated to your fellow commentators and stuff like that. So it's okay.

V95   Obviously your voice plays such an important role in commentating. Do you do anything to prepare your voice? Or to prepare in general?

ICT   I think a lot of people do. For me personally, I've been doing it so long, and my day-to-day back at home is very *StarCraft*-centric or commentary-centric anyways as a streamer, so my voice is usually in pretty peak condition and my knowledge base is readily available. And I don't branch out too much. So I'm just naturally prepared for it.

V95   Commentating live is usually done by two people at once. Can you talk a little bit about what makes that co-commentator rhythm work?

ICT   Yeah, the thing to avoid as a commentating duo

is stepping on each other's toes: interrupting, cutting in, and dominating the microphone too much. That can feel crowded or you get a little bit awkward, right? Because then the hand-offs become kind of unpredictable and strange. The best commentary situations, I've found, are the ones where you're really familiar with the person, and you can make each other laugh. You can discuss things organically and seem to be very friendly. Oftentimes, with us in the *StarCraft* crew, we are very friendly. We're all good friends and enjoy each other's company.

Generally, there's a balance between one person being more of a hype person [and the other taking a deeper, more analytic look at what's happening]. For example, during a big battle, it's not quite as important to break down the economy. Instead you've got to make it sound very exciting, and get very energetic and vocal about it, so that you can raise the emotion a bit. Then the other commentator, typically, will break that up with a deeper look into what's going on in the game.

V95   Interesting. How would you say that balance between a hype person and a more analytic person came about?

ICT   I think it's more that people just got better at it [over time]. It's basically a science of what makes for a good casting duo. It doesn't have to be rigid. But what's been pretty clearly demonstrated across gaming, and into sports as well, is that if two people do exactly the same thing, that tends to be a lesser tier of broadcasting. So one person generally slides into the role of making things exciting and being loud, and the other into the role of asking more analytical questions.

V95   You've been playing for more than 15 years. How would describe how the gameplay of *StarCraft* has changed over the years?

ICT   I think the only answer I could give is how impos-

Geoff "iNcontroLTV" Robinson

Video Games

STREAMING IS SOCIAL BUT, AT THE SAME TIME, YOU'RE NOT SEEING PEOPLE'S FACES, YOU'RE NOT HEARING THEIR VOICES. YOU'RE WATCHING NAMES ON THE SIDE-SCROLLING CHAT WINDOW.

Geoff "iNcontroLTV" Robinson

sibly large that question is. *StarCraft II* has been around for nine years. *StarCraft* and *StarCraft: Brood War* have been around over 20 years and in that time the meta has shifted so dramatically and so tremendously that it would be impossible to track it in a conversation. All I can tell you is that the beauty of this game is that the skill ceiling is actually impossible. Nobody has perfected the game. It's not even doable. Right now, a supercomputer, AI, is attempting to do that; it's playing more games than the combined number of games every human on earth has ever played, and it still hasn't perfected the game, so...

> Video Games will be seen for what they really are, the most advanced and emotionally stirring art form. Not only do they combine all other forms of art in themselves, they introduce gameplay and mechanics as a part of the art.
> In all forms of art you observe and feel via surrogate. In video games, YOU will feel, there is no obfuscation in the experience of the art. As technology advances, that obfuscation will lessen and lessen until video game experiences are nearly indistinguishable from reality.

V95   Are you optimistic for the future of the game?

ICT   Well, last year we experienced an increase in growth across the board, in terms of player base, viewership, and just about every kind of metric. That's really weird for a game in its eighth year. I'm not about to tell you that it's going to replace *Apex*, or *Fortnite*, or *League of Legends*, or anything like that. But I will tell you that, as pretty much the last modern RTS to be played actively and competitively, it's doing very, very well. It's aged like a fine wine, and that's exciting.

Am I excited about the future? I'm a little apprehensive. Blizzard itself seems to be a little bit unstable. Also, in the gaming market, if you're not number one, you might as well be last. *StarCraft* is not number one, and it's very hard for *StarCraft* to get a lot of sponsorships or excite people the way it used to. It's doing very well, but because it's not top two or three, to some people it might as well be dead. It's hard to tell you with a straight face that the future is extremely bright, but what I would tell you is that, for the people who are enjoying the game, we have a robust circuit of professional tournaments, we have a huge player base, and we have the best game we've ever had. We are backed by Blizzard; they're supporting us tremendously through the War Chest and other initiatives, and it's really great.

V95   Do you see professional league eSports becoming more popular in the States in the future?

ICT   Oh, yeah. It's inevitable. With every five, ten years, you can absolutely feel it. We are the generation that grew up playing games, and I'm kind of at that forefront a little bit. We're the people that had Nintendo 64s and PlayStations as kids. We played *Age of Empires*. We booted up our modems and played *Counter-Strike* 1.6. We grew up playing video games, and a lot of those games that we played were social and competitive. So as time moves forward, these people become, like I am, 30 but then 40 and 50, and our money starts to translate into owning companies and having influence over raising our young, that kind of stuff. We will support the content we want and start watching the things we want. You can already see it. Cable television's at an all-time low. Basically, SportsCenter and ESPN are the only things keeping it afloat right now, but even they're reporting losses. People are filling up Madison Square Garden. They're traveling across the country. They're traveling across the world to go and watch gaming events. It's just happening. It's just going to happen no matter what, whether the people like it or not, and I think that's exciting and fun because at the end of the day if you don't like it, you don't have to watch it; but if you *do,* it's taking bigger and bigger stages, which is always exciting.

V95   It's pretty cool to be alive during this transformation, which is so new. It's so massive, so unique. Let's pivot to your streaming. How long have you been streaming? How long have you been partnered on Twitch? And how's your experience with Twitch been?

ICT   That's also been quite the interesting transformation to witness from my perspective. I streamed on Twitch back when it was called Justin.tv. Back then you basically just made an account, and made sure you could stream, and boom, you were doing it. There were no subscribers at the very beginning, There were no "bits" or anything like that. You just ran advertisements and made pretty good money doing that. It was just amazing because, at the time, streaming took this social aspect of gaming and expanded it even more. Back in 2010/11, when I was first getting into streaming as a main source of income, you would stream to 4, 5, 6, 10 thousand people. That would add this exciting exhibitionist element to the gameplay. A lot of people are very private, and that's nice too, but when you have 5,000 people cheering you on, it's something else.

I've been streaming since about 2010 but the beast has changed so much. Now, you make almost no money from advertisements. You make most of it from subs and donations and bits and sponsorships. And now there are also people who are not just streaming games because they want to stream games, but who are thinking, "Twitch is how I want to make my living." That's not a good or bad thing, it's just different; it changes the name of the game. There are thousands and thousands of partners now, whereas when I was streaming it was hundreds. It's fun to watch it become its own animal.

V95   How many hours would you say that you stream a week? Do you have a schedule? How do you allocate time to it?

ICT   That's a tough one to answer. This week, for instance, I'm at home, so I would tell you I stream anywhere between three to eight hours a day. One of my favorite parts of being a streamer is that I'm my own boss. So if on

Friday my buddy wants to come over and play *Warhammer*, or, if I'm just really tired from a long week or something like that I'll be like, "You know what? I'll stream for a couple hours, but then I'm going to watch some shows, go to the gym, hang out, go see a movie or something like that. I'm going to take it easy." And I think that's something that steamers have to be very aware of. You can very easily just be indoors, Amazon-ordering stuff and streaming for ten hours a day, but you'll find yourself in a big rut. I go to the gym every day. I break up my streams. I don't stream for huge, ten-hour blocks. I stream for four or five hours at the most and then go have lunch or something. I try to do the best I can to keep myself very healthy. But I guess, on average, if I'm home I stream something like 50 hours a week.

V95 Do you still game with friends socially? Does steaming ever get lonely?

ICT I think it would be a lonely experience if you only ever streamed. Streaming is social but, at the same time, you're not seeing people's

I imagine video games would be pretty close to extended virtual reality. Think Matrix, and being plugged into a machine generated simulation.

I think vidya will be mostly mobile. People will still play but nobody will care.

Same as today!

They could be for art, leisure, or health (VR physical therapy).

It's going to be more of the same, just more intensely so. Maybe more immersive, maybe a little more postmodern.

It will be the entirety of existence for some humans.

They'll continue to serve as a source of entertainment and enjoyment, and on top of that, with the rise of streaming platforms and games like VRChat, will become an increasing source of community.

faces, you're not hearing their voices. You're watching names on the side-scrolling chat window. It's not really a full-on social experience. That's why I break up my day and do a whole bunch of different things. I try and do things on weekends. Maybe I'll play some other things, some retro gaming that I'm not streaming. Just nice and relaxed, window open, breeze coming through, and enjoying that.

V95   Are you worried that Twitch will just become a place where people try to get rich playing games?

ICT   No. It definitely happens, but I wouldn't describe myself as worried. But I do speak to countless people who are trying to force becoming a professional streamer. Usually what happens is that gaming has been an escape for them, but now they're trying to monetize it. And, of course, if it takes longer than expected to get viewers they can become resentful of this thing that they used to do for fun. It's kind of like going into business with your friend. You have the chance to ruin that friendship. It's a tough animal.

V95   Totally. Are you worried about the number of viewers you have when you're streaming? And does that affect how your perform?

ICT   I think the broad answer is absolutely, it does. Anyone that tells you otherwise is not being honest or is not really fully aware, I suppose. If I have 5,000 people watching I definitely pep it up a bit. You know, you lean into it because it's a big opportunity. My average viewership is anywhere between 500 and 1,000 people, plus or minus, you know, depending on what's going on.

V95   Which is basically the size of a Broadway theater.

ICT   Yeah. It's pretty good. It's a pretty good audience. And my brand, and the way I have forged my career, is that I don't want to act abnormal. I don't want to force a *character* on people or anything like that. So I just kind of be myself. It's definitely not what I think you should do to have the maximum viewership, but for me it keeps me mentally sane and happy and enjoying what I do. That's the kind of happy, healthy medium I'm trying to walk, basically.

V95   A recurring comment from everybody that we've talked to who's into streaming, particularly, is that you can't expect success to happen overnight, and that you've got to find some sort of balance between personal and professional life, otherwise it's just going to be a burnout.

ICT   Yeah. Because your stream is your business you can do it whenever, right? It's a little bit poisonous that way. When you play a game, you're like, "Well, why aren't I streaming it?" and also, "Geez, I only streamed for five hours? I could stream for more and make more money and grow my viewership." If you're worried about all those things it can bleed into your psyche and just constantly be there.

V95   What's up for you in five years? Where do you see your career moving? Anything in particular you're pursuing?

ICT   You know, I think what's really cool is that I have some nice pathfinders in front of me. People like djWHEAT, SirScoots, and even Redeye. Some of these guys are 10 years older than me and are still doing this kind of stuff. So the idea that you can only do gaming up to a certain age is not really true. But what's been fun, for me, is that I don't really need to think of my career in terms of, "Where do I go from here?" It's more of a, "This is working, I'm excited about this, lets keep going." And now I'm also working more with Games Workshop, which is a company I've loved since I was 12. So, for right now, I don't think about my future. I don't think about what I need to focus on doing to secure my future. It's more of just enjoying the way it is. I'm on it right now.

V95   Sounds good. Anything to add?

ICT   Well, I think the only thing I would add... It's almost a dead horse that we're beating, but it still seems to be a big topic. A lot of people think of gaming as a mindless activity that you do in lieu of something else, but I like to think that what's been really fun—and hopefully this collection of interviews encompasses and shows this—is that I could not imagine my life without gaming. Gaming has traveled me around the world and enriched my life tremendously. It's introduced me to amazing people. It's given me worldly experience. It's given me business acumen. It's allowing me to be a public speaker, an educator. All these things that I want out of life have been done through gaming. If you look at most of the games now they're all social, right? You're all playing with people, against people, or alongside people. If you're not, then you're visiting websites, and you're going on to chats where you're talking about games with other people. So it's just this huge social phenomenon that connects us to people across the world, and I think if you're a person that's not a part of gaming or hasn't really looked into it, it may be interesting to think about it in those terms, because it's come a long way.

Geoff "INcontroLTV" Robinson

How much do you agree or disagree with the following statement: "People often play video games to avoid feeling lonely."

10.3

2.8

10.1

23.2

Strongly disagree: 2.8%
Disagree: 10.1%
Neutral: 28.2%
Agree: 39.6%
Strongly agree: 19.3%

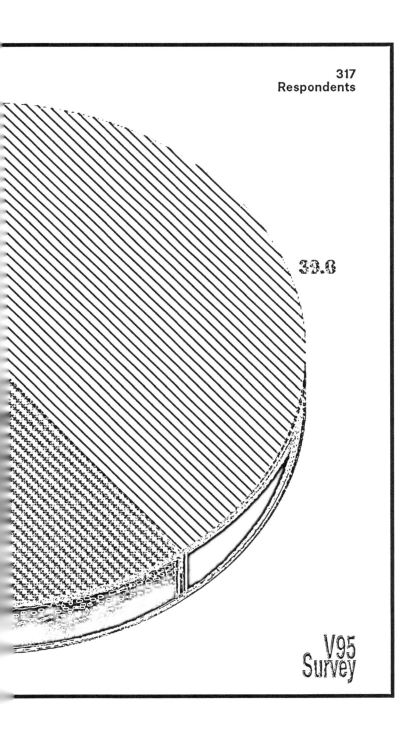

33.6

V95
Survey

Video

ZombiUnicorn

Natalie Casanova

V95   How do you describe what you do for a living?

ZU   Well, whenever I'm taking an Uber or something, the first thing I say is, "I play video games professionally." But, I do a lot more than just play video games professionally, and I don't necessarily play them at a professional level all the time. I am an online personality who creates content about gaming. There's a professional aspect to what I do. All my production is super high quality. I use the best equipment I can. I'm always upgrading—upgrading equipment is a hobby of mine. I've been doing this full time for five years, and I've been streaming for almost seven. And it's my career, so I do everything: streaming live on Twitch, creating content for YouTube, posting on various social media platforms... I also do voice acting. And I host events on TV, usually related to the fields of gaming and technology.

V95   How did you find streaming in particular? What was your first experience of streaming?

ZU   My first experience was in 2012. *Smite,* by Hi-Rez Studios was in closed beta at the time. It was really, really fun. I loved how all the characters in the game were based on mythology. And I just really wanted to get good at the game. So I watched a lot of streams, and I found one streamer in particular who was very engaging and interesting, and very down to earth. I basically just became a part of his community. I would play with him and other people and I got a lot better at the game. Then one day he was like,

"Hey, you know what? Why don't you throw your camera on Skype? And I'll put your camera on my stream as well." So I did that and people were really warm and welcoming to me on camera. So next he said, "You know what? You should start your own stream." So I did.

Shortly afterwards, Hi-Rez studios reached out to me to stream *Smite* officially on their channel. That got me a lot of traction as well. A lot of people started hearing about me, so I branched out to other games and I started doing YouTube. Now I mainly do Twitch because it's just so hard to do both. But basically, I just really wanted to get better at this one game, and that snowballed into a lot of other things.

V95   When Hi-Rez got in touch with you, is that when you decided that maybe this is a career?

ZU   No, no, not yet. They didn't pay us back then. We didn't realize that we should have been getting paid for creating content for them. We were just excited to be featured! It wasn't until I got partnered on Twitch that I realized I could do it as a job.

V95   You mentioned that you like upgrading your equipment. What was your first streaming system?

ZU   The very first computer I streamed from was my boyfriend-at-the-time's computer. Then I quickly built my own PC. I built the cheapest, crappiest, shittiest computer I could that would run games. It was so funny, because I had never built a PC before. It's really not that hard!

V95   I was going to say, I've always been kind of terrified of building my own PC. It's not hard?

ZU   I've always been very DIY. I'm always like, "You know what? If there's a guide out there on how to do it, I can tackle it. I can do it." [That PC was crappy but] it was perfect! It could barely stream and play games at the same time, but yeah, I used that for a while.

V95	The DIY, kinda scrappy look fits your aesthetic well. And then I'm assuming you upgraded your PC at some point?

ZU	I've always had a unique look. I've always had this bright pink hair, and I have a very no-BS attitude—that's always been something that's helped me stand out. When I was partnered on Twitch I ended up picking up a PC sponsor, and they sent me a better PC, and I streamed off of that for a while. Then I was sponsored by NVIDIA for a while. I helped them launch their channel, and they sent me a new PC. I use a two-PC setup now, one to game and one to stream and capture the gaming PC and do all the other stuff. The gaming PC is a sponsored rig as well from Origin PC. I've been very fortunate to not have to build any computers anymore...

V95	Can you walk us through a bit of how you managed to grow the career you have now? Were you always thinking about streaming and creating for YouTube as a business with long term goals?

ZU	Yeah, kind of. I used to really enjoy making YouTube videos. I got in with this group of people who liked playing games a certain way and recording them. So I got into that habit. Then I started streaming as well... I was doing streaming and YouTube full-time, which is very hard to keep up. A lot of people do it—they [take] highlights [from streams] and put them on their YouTube channel. To me it's so exhausting...
	I went to college for a couple different things. I first went for music theory and composition. I was studying classical guitar, and then I dropped out. Then I went back for journalism. I was the editor-in-chief of my college paper. I loved creating what [at the time] we called "new media." Back then what we called "new media" was video content and interviews. So when I was first doing YouTube I did

interviews at conventions and things like that. Interviews with game developers—more journalistic content. I guess now, to this day, whenever I pick up a new game (or get a review copy) I'll play it and stream it and basically do a live review. But it's more of a *fun* live review. It's definitely less journalistic.

I've cultivated an audience over the years and I've been very lucky to have an audience that enjoys watching me play whatever game I feel like playing, as long as I'm having fun. They just seem to enjoy my personality first and foremost. They may not have even have heard of the game I'm playing.

V95   Absolutely. When you were doing the full-fledged YouTube plus Twitch schedule, how many hours a week was that? What did your day-to-day look like in those days?

ZU   Well, I did Twitch and YouTube full-time for a few years. It's a constant job just to be a streamer [in part because] you have to be involved in social media. Some people are successful without really using Twitter or Instagram. But I like to have my hand in every basket. I like to do a little Instagram. I like to do a little Twitter. I like to have options. I'm constantly on social media checking stuff out, keeping up to date, trying to see what's the newest trend in gaming.

Back then, when I was doing both full time, it was at least 60 to 70 hours a week of actual sitting down and working, not to mention being on my phone all the time. I think I just got really depressed... I got depressed because I didn't leave my room a lot and I didn't have much of a life outside of gaming. Even the guy I was dating was long distance... So it was just really depressing. I had to stop. I had to get more of a "real life" balance. Now, I still work a lot. I work 40 plus hours a week, but not all of it is streaming. Usually, when I stream, I stream a minimum of three hours, and then sometimes I'll stream up to 10 hours in one session. I used to do 24-hour streams all the time and that was

just exhausting. I'm getting too old for that. I try to save those for special occasions, like charity streams and stuff. I'm doing a lot of behind-the-scenes work at the moment; updating my graphics, tweaking stuff, working on new collaborations, planning content, doing more voice acting, planning conventions... It's a lot of boring paperwork and email-type stuff now. More off-platform stuff, because it helps me keep a better real life balance.

V95   Do you feel like you're yourself when you're on screen? Are you acting? Are you a persona? Is it some-

Natalie "ZombiUnicorn" Casanova

where in between?

ZU I'm myself. I know a lot of people put on a character. There are some people who are very blatantly characters. You have your FuturemanGaming, your DrDisrespects,
people like that. Then there are some people who are just
more subtly a character. They're the people who would
say [privately], "I would never say this on stream..." I'm the
type of person who'd rather be like, "I'll say it. I'll say it on
stream. If this is how I'm feeling, I will say it..." Let me put
it this way: if I have nothing nice to say about something,

I will either not say anything at all, or I will just give a very respectful statement explaining why I don't like it. Other than that, I'm exactly myself. I'm not any different on camera than I am off. The only difference is that I might have a coffee before I stream, so my energy level is at an 11 rather than a 7. But basically, it's the same.

V95   It seems like that kind of honesty must help to grow a relationship with the community that follows you. Do you actively participate in the chat? Are you in touch with your fans in other ways?

ZU   I do have a community Discord. I talk to them on Twitter and Instagram, stuff like that. In general I'm super active with the chat. I play a lot of games where I'm able to stop and just have a conversation, rather than focus on the game. But then, when I start playing a game where I need to focus there will be times where somebody will get upset and be like, "Streamer, pay attention to me!" I'll be in the middle of trying to kill someone in-game [and can't stop for the chat]! It's a balance. They'll be like, "Streamer, pay attention to me. Streamer, stop sucking at the game. Streamer..." It's hard to do both sometimes.

V95   Are you in touch with other streamers in the broader community of Twitch or YouTube content creators? Do you guys hang out IRL?

ZU   I'm a social butterfly, and I'm a big extrovert, but I have a lot of introverted tendencies. Having been on Twitch for so long, I know a lot of streamers. I also know a lot of people in the YouTube community because I was on YouTube creating content regularly back in the old days when it was a lot smaller and more tight-knit. I don't follow YouTube as much anymore. It's blown up. There are so many content creators I've never even heard of.
     I do love living in LA. I moved here for my career, so I could have more real-life collaborations and opportunities. One of the reasons I like living here is because

the general mood and attitude is that people want to go outside and hang out with other people. The other creators here, (there are a lot of the YouTube creators here), like going out and hanging out in real life. That's something I needed in my life: the balance, instead of just sitting in a room gaming 24/7. I do hang out with a lot of people here, usually weekly.

V95   Twitch and YouTube both, it would seem, have really blown up. They're very exciting platforms, but not without their darker corners. How would you assess the general Twitch ecosystem? Do you think there are issues that the platform needs to address? How would you assess Twitch right now?

ZU   I've been on Twitch for so long. Long before Amazon owned it. I've seen it change so much. I think Amazon did a really good job of not changing Twitch too quickly, and I think a lot of the changes have been for the better. For example, there's this thing called the Bounty Board, which is essentially a way to do brand deals with different video games, or products, or TV shows. It has a simple way of tracking [the deal], then we get paid per average viewers. It's somehow a nice way of making streaming more of a career without the middleman of a manager or an agent or something like that. I do have a manager and an agent as well, and I work on different stuff with them, but Twitch has made strides in trying to make it a more sustainable career for their streamers. They've created things we've been asking for for years. I can remember asking Twitch for gifted subs in 2014. Subscriptions *drive* a channel. I remember asking for that in 2014 and then just last year we got gifted subs.

I think it's easier than ever to get partnered, as long as you put in the work and have something to offer. Quality content, unique content. Streaming is not for everybody. Just because you're a really nice person and you have fun playing video games doesn't mean you have that certain spark, unfortunately. I think everybody should go into it with the intention of having fun, and if it picks up for you, you can make a plan and find a way to continue. That's always my piece of advice.

V95   It's been a recurring theme in these interviews that streaming is never an instant career.

ZU   Be reserved in who you trust, just like in real life and business. You have to cultivate a community and you have to grow over time. It took me a long time to get where I am. I'm not the greatest example. I've been inconsistent. I don't stream all the time, as I should. I've never had a schedule. The only time I had a schedule was when I was streaming for somebody else's channel. If I had had a schedule, if I was more consistent, I'd probably be a lot more famous, more successful than I am now. But I have this balance that I have to maintain to be happy as a person. For me, it's important to remember to just have fun. If you don't feel like streaming that day, or you're not having a good time and you don't want to fake it, then don't.

V95   You mentioned that you had asked Twitch for gifted subs. Do you think streamers should play a more active role in shaping how the platform is designed and how it works day-to-day?

ZU   Well, Twitch does a lot of research. And what better way to find out what's going to help their streamers than asking the streamers themselves? I've consulted for Twitch countless times over the last five plus years. Ever since I've been a partner, they've asked me a lot of questions about how I feel about things. I consulted for their mobile app for streaming, for example.

V95   So you have a really active dialogue with them?

ZU   Yeah. I don't know if everybody has that with them, but I've been somebody who's been very proactive over the years. Especially with the way they handle their terms

THEY [...] SEEM TO ENJOY MY PERSONALITY FIRST AND FOREMOST. THEY MAY NOT HAVE EVEN HAVE HEARD OF THE GAME I'M PLAYING.

Natalie "ZombiUnicorn' Casanova

of service and how people are allowed to treat others on a platform.

Coming from journalism, I'm very passionate about social issues—people can call me a social justice warrior, whatever. I understand how funny a politically incorrect joke can be sometimes. I'm not a hardcore "no fun" person. But at the same time, I do feel Twitch should be a place where everybody is comfortable.

I've been somebody who's definitely been more proactive on Twitch. Like, if somebody comes into my chat saying, "Get back in the kitchen, blah, blah, blah, blah," they shouldn't be able to do that. That's not okay. I don't think that's funny. Those are the kinds of jokes I would see constantly over the years. No matter what I wore, I would still get nasty, awful things said to me. So I've been very proactive in discouraging that language. I've met so many women and people in the LGBT community who say, "I don't feel like streaming anymore because I hate getting all these nasty, hurtful things said to me."

Before they put out the new terms of service last year Twitch reached out to some partners, including me, for feedback on the new rules. It was exciting to see some of the things that were changing and whatnot. But, I think they do still have a long way to go and I'm very grateful that they consider how their creators feel, even as such a big company.

V95   I get the sense that the Twitch community is a bit closer and tighter knit than then YouTube community.

ZU   Twitch is definitely a big family—a big, dysfunctional family, sure, but it's still a big family. We all bleed purple, as we like to say! There's a big sense of community among Twitch. That's why I think TwitchCon is probably my favorite gaming convention. I love E3 and everything but TwitchCon is more about the community. Even if there are people you don't know, you're like, "Oh, I've heard of them before." And, "Hey, they look like they hang out with somebody else I like, and I know, and I watch. Maybe they're cool, too." On YouTube everybody kind of stays in their lane for the most part. You don't have this thing where you go raid another channel when you're done watching a video, unless you're doing a collaboration with another YouTuber. On Twitch it's like, "I'm done streaming. You guys are still here so let's go find somebody to host and you guys can go watch them." We all kind of share these viewers and just spread the love constantly.

V95   That's a nice sentiment. Given that this is a relatively new profession and you're one of its first very successful professionals, what do you see the next five years of your stream being like? And how do you see Twitch evolving in the future?

ZU   Well, I can't see the future, but one thing that I have always done is tried to upgrade the quality of my stream. I've been using a DSLR instead of a webcam for about three years now, and I originally wrote the guide on how to do that and helped a lot of streamers set up their streams to do the same. I'm not trying to claim anything, but I definitely was big in starting that trend of getting higher quality cameras going.

There are big channels with multiple camera angles, and beautiful graphics, and sets, and things like that. But those are usually company-run community channels. I'm a one-man band. I'm trying to get to that level on my own with no help. I run everything on my own thanks to various equipment like the Stream Deck and the GoXLR mixer. Anyway, I want to be more interactive, and to always have a higher-quality stream. That's the future for me and my channel. Content-wise it's always changing so I can't really guess just yet. It's just constant research: try something new, see if it works, keep going with the same stuff that is working, and whatnot.

Other than that, I think some people are creating really cool characters and using graphics in cool ways. I just watched another streamer the other day who has this whole cardboard cowboy bit. He doesn't have a great

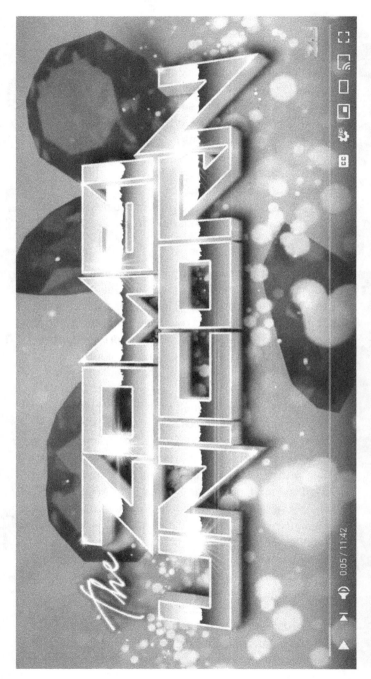

HE WANTS MY TACO! ("Sims 4" | ep. 1)

webcam or anything but he has production quality. He has a bunch of scenes with different pictures overlaid and he switches scenes very quickly and it makes it look like he's this animated cardboard guy! It's really funny, and it's really cute, and it's very unique.

V95   What are you playing right now, and what are you excited about in video games at the moment?

ZU   Oh boy. [Laughter.] I feel, like everybody else, I've been playing a lot of *Apex Legends*. It's so much fun, but for me it's because I was a huge *Titanfall 1* and *2* fan. A lot of

---

Influence people and how they act towards others. I.e kind and gentle.

I think that games will be as they are right now, so essentially just another form of entertainment like watching movies and reading books. I do think that games will be pretty much rooted online and that there will be more emphasis on artistic integrity with singleplayer games.

It's going to take on a much larger role in mainstream storytelling and entertainment in general. It has shown to be an extremely adaptable medium over the years.

Have you seen ready player one? Yeah like that

by 2069 we will have discovered that the world itself is a video game with Elon Musk as the protagonist

Girls will play

It will be the main stay hang out space. Enough people have met their best friends online, it'll only become more common and more accepted

I think video games will be an escape from reality.

I'm still gonna be alone playing them, so...

They will become more intense and imbedded in modern culture of the year 2068.

Idk lmao

people were really turned off by *Titanfall* 1 back in the day. And so not a lot of people jumped into *Titanfall 2*, but I absolutely loved it. I worked with EA on promoting it because I loved it so much. It's set in the same world. It has a lot of the same mechanics, and I just absolutely love it. I'm terrible at it—getting better—but it's still fun for me. I really am glad that it's doing so well because that just means more money for Respawn to create. It backs up Respawn as a developer. Now they can definitely put out a *Titanfall 3*, which I'm really excited for! I think they've kind of announced that they're doing it, but there's no roadmap or anything yet.

V95 Have you emailed them already to say you're available for promotions? [Laughter.]

ZU Oh, yeah. I'm all over it. It's funny because I always joke about people being like, "Oh, I love *Titanfall*." I'm like, "Oh, do you though [laughter]? Or are you just jumping on the *Apex* bandwagon?" I'm

---

I think videogames will appeal to almost every live generation, as the generation they appeal to now will be one of the oldest. They will definitely improve in quality but, like today, a lot of games will be very well made, but UNORIGINAL or slightly dull even, but every once in awhile a genuinely good game, with real substance, meaning, and thoughtfulness, no matter how simple will come out. (Examples: Minecraft, Undertale, FNaF)

Prolly about the sams

Same as today probably

They will be the new football, the new basketball, the new SPORTS.

It'll be similar to today, widely popular and cultural staples. But the big difference will be the few of the older generations. Since they grew up on them, older generations will be more accepting of video games than the older generations of today.

Same role as now but more stimulating, addicting and advanced. Also more money involved.

> I think video games will become an integral part of daily life and will consume all forms of media, i.e. sports, entertainment, news, etc.
>
> I think games are a form of entertainment just like music and movies have been for years, but are now coming to the forefront of society and people are beginning to appreciate their artistic value. I feel like video games are only going to get better and better with time.

not a gatekeeper, but I like to poke fun because people used to make fun of me for loving *Titanfall 2*. I didn't care. It's like an ongoing joke in my channel. So *Apex Legends* is one, and then the other game that's probably not coming out for a while that looks really cool and exciting is *Cyberpunk 2077* from CD Projekt Red. That game looks insane and amazing, and I just cannot wait. I have to wait for a while, but once it comes out, it'll be amazing.

V95   Anything else on your mind?

ZU   Sure. I think that it's important to remember, at the end of the day, if somebody is not being very nice to you online, you don't have to take what they're saying to heart. They don't really know you. And they're a human being on the other side of that keyboard. They're probably not having the best day or the best life. They're probably just taking stuff out on you. It's been hard for me to learn how to deal with that properly and respectfully, but I think it's an important thing to remember. Try not to take trolls' mean comments to heart. And just try your best to be nice! We all definitely get a little hurt when we read mean comments online. The more love and positivity we can spread online, the better we can make it for everybody.

Over the next five years, do you expect the quality of video games being produced to get better, worse, stay the same, or you aren't sure?

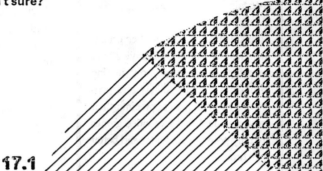

11.4

17.1

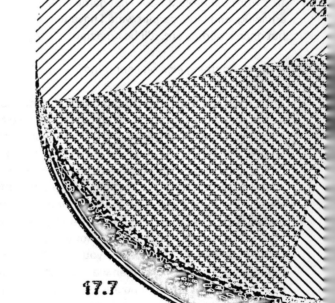

17.7

Better: 53.8%
Worse: 11.4%
Stay the same: 17.1 %
Not sure: 17.7%

63.0

**V95
Survey**

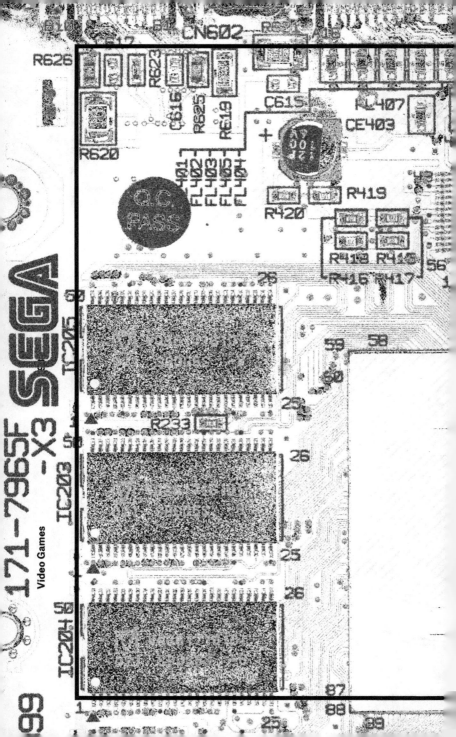

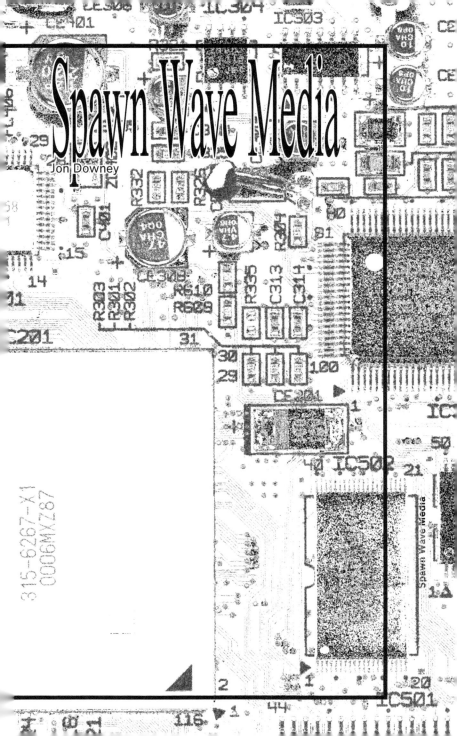

Spawn Wave Media

Jon Downey

This conversation with
news outlet
Spawn Wave Media (Jonathan Downey)
was recorded 2/8/19

V95   When did you decide to start getting into YouTube?

SWM   It was actually around the time when the [Nintendo] Switch was starting to get revealed. I was interested in the technology behind it—I had been following the Tegra processor for so long and I wanted it to go into a game console, and it finally did. So I became very, very interested in creating content explaining the idea and the specs of the Switch, and it kind of turned into me providing news, or summaries of news, every day. And then from there, it turned into me tearing down different consoles; explaining them, how they work, and why the system may have succeeded in the past, or what made it different and special from other things around it. So it kind of went from explanations of technology to news and then to history and technology, but it worked out really well. And the nice thing about YouTube is that basically anyone can do it. You don't have to go through trying to be an intern at a TV station, just to eventually get on air 10 to 15 years later, after you've spent X amount of years basically getting the coffee. [Laughter.] You can set up a camera, and you can just put your passion out there. So I think YouTube—or just online media—is the future, in general. I think cable-cutting is happening right now just because of that.

V95   Was your intention always to build this into something that could be a career, a profession? Or did this start as a real labor of love and accidentally became something like that?

SWM Oh, no. At first it was just me in my basement with a camcorder, basically just having fun, and from there it turned into something that is, at this point, a self-sustainable business. But it's nice because it's stuff I enjoy doing—I have relationships with a lot of the bigger game companies to the point where I can get press releases right away from them, which helps with the news bit. They'll send me the games to check out ahead of time. It's turned from, yeah, someone in their basement with a camcorder into someone who is essentially running a business at their house.

V95 What have significant milestones been for you? Was there a specific moment when you thought, "Wow, I could really do this. I could really turn this into this business?"

SWM I mean, obviously when you start getting subscribers, that helps a lot. But I think it was when bigger YouTube channels started recognizing what I was doing. We have a podcast that we do on the weekends and, at one point, one of the bigger channels, The Know, actually started reporting on stuff we were talking about—

V95 —Is the podcast you are referring to *SpawnCast*?

SWM Yeah, *SpawnCast*. The Know started picking up some of the stuff we were doing, and it was really cool—I mean, they're part of Rooster Teeth and everything.

The biggest thing that really made me think I could actually do something with the channel was when the Switch first came out and there were issues with the Joy-Con controller. I remember I opened it up for one of my videos to show off the insides of it, and I noticed that there was an issue with the antenna placement. So I soldered a cable to the antenna point on the board, ran it down to the bottom, and it actually fixed the issue. And YouTube actually put me on Trending at the time because of it, so the video accrued hundreds of thousands of views, a lot of new people came by, and at that point it was basically full speed ahead.

V95 Did you get any reaction from Nintendo for that video?

SWM No, Nintendo never really reached out to me, outside of just some people on Twitter talking about it. But they did seemingly recognize that there was an issue with the Joy-Con, as they eventually let you send it in and get it back with a fix. And when people opened it up, [Nintendo] had put a foam block over that area—so rather than reroute the antenna, they basically just insulated it—so there was some admittance that there was a problem.

V95 How did you decide to do start scheduling your daily news program, *News Wave*, 8am?

SWM The idea at first was to just do it every now and then, as news popped up. But I was also noticing that some people would schedule their [uploads]. At the time notifications on YouTube were spotty, so I figured that if I scheduled [each episode] in the morning—at 8am—people didn't even need the notification: they would just know where to go. And that's worked out really well, to the point where I actually recommend that people starting with YouTube do it… because if you can schedule things, you don't have to worry about people just seeing [your videos] by chance or rely on YouTube to send a notification. It's hard because I have to make sure I have a video up and ready to go the night before and scheduled for

Metroid Inspired Jedi Fallen Order And Did A New Nvidia...

33K views · 10 hours ago

Animal Crossing's Confusing Decision Annoys Fans And...

72K views · 1 day ago

The Nintendo Switch Has A TON Of Games Coming Out...

92K views · 4 days ago

More Zelda Breath Of The Wild 2 Details From E3 And...

99K views · 4 days ago

The BIG Change Coming To Super Mario Maker 2 And...

68K views · 6 days ago

Nintendo Just Dominated E3 2019

96K views · 1 week ago

8am, but I actually think it's helped the channel drastically. It's basically like what TV is, just on YouTube, because we know when our favorite shows will be on. Back in the day, I still remember when *The Simpsons* was on on a Thursday night.

V95   Funny, so do I.

SWM   So yeah, scheduling *News Wave* was probably one of the best changes I made. And that happened about four months or so after I started.

V95   Yeah, I mean, the fact that I know when I know to expect it keeps me coming back. I usually watch you over breakfast. [Laughter.]

SWM   There you go! People tell me they usually eat breakfast—or lunch, depending on their time zone—or they'll be listening on the drive to work.

V95   So you have the daily *News Wave*, and you have the *SpawnCast* on Saturdays; and on top of that you have *Rumor Wave*, where you talk about rumors flying around the industry, and *Tech Wave*, where you open up pieces of gaming hardware to see how things are put together. Does one of these programs best represent the channel?

SWM   I know people like *News Wave* a lot. I actually really like *Tech Wave*. The thing about *Tech Wave* is that it takes longer to make [each episode]. Especially now. For example, I just did a [*Tech Wave*] video that did really well, and that was because I spent a bit more time trying to flesh out the history of [the thing I was taking apart]. I've decided to start leaning more on that, rather than just the quick and dirty teardown part of the video. But [*Tech Wave*] is the one I think is most representative because it's a bit of history, it's a bit of news, and then it's a bit of a tech teardown, all in one.

V95   I'd love to know more about behind the scenes at *Spawn Wave*. Specifically, what kind of equipment you are using and what your weekly schedule looks like.

SWM   Oh, sure. I mean, it's a Monday to Sunday kind of thing to be honest. [Laughter.] It's basically every day. But the nice thing is that you work from home, so it doesn't feel as much like work. and because I'm working with technology and gaming, it feels even less like work. I have my wife and son at home and, if I want to see them or say "hi," I just walk upstairs, or sometimes they'll just come down here.
     For the equipment stuff: I have three computers and a laptop, basically, and several game consoles (of

course), and a full green screen—like a 6x8 green screen—and four studio lights. I know people get concerned about getting into YouTube because it's expensive but, to be honest, I started with a $200 camcorder from Walmart. So [laughter] if you want to start, you can. The best piece of advice I could give is: get a mic first. Get a Blue Snowball for $50 and just voice over video to get started. Then buy equipment as your channel or passion grows, rather than just trying to take out a loan and buying everything at once. I would say I work with a medium-tier amount of equipment. I don't have the RED camera or anything. In fact, the camera I still use is a Panasonic G7 and that's like a $500 camera.

V95   Can YouTube even support a RED's output?

SWM   Yeah, actually, a lot of the bigger guys use RED cameras. I know Tech Tips, Marques Brownlee, they all have RED cameras. And the reason is that, while YouTube supports 4K right now, it doesn't support 8K. So these guys are more thinking about the future. If YouTube decides to upgrade to 8K, all they have to do is re-upload the video, or maybe because they've uploaded an 8K video it will just tick up to 8K.

V95   What's the schedule for making a single *News Wave* episode?

SWM   Usually I'll start in the morning, generally between 9am and 10am... I get a lot press releases in the morning. Some of it's embargo, some of it's not—"embargo" means that I have to hold the information until X date. Sometimes I'll get a press release one day in advance. More usually I'll get a press release hours in advance and that will give me a chance to put it in the episode. Otherwise, throughout the day, I usually use Google Drive so I can work on multiple computers, and I go around finding news stories that I can research. Once I have a nice list, it basically ends up looking like an outline that you'd make for a paper in college or something, where you have topics, bullet points, and then full written parts of research, dates, prices, sources... After I have that all set up I'll start filming. I usually edit at night to get it done for the next morning. And then it's scheduled and ready to go.

V95   Are you writing the script to read through verbatim, or are these bullet points? And do you use a teleprompter?

SWM   No, actually, they're all bullet points. I do have a teleprompter so I can see what bullet points I have to hit, and then I also have a laptop underneath the camera—so I have a couple of screens of information. At that point, I kind of just go and form the words as I roll along. So it's more of a conversation, rather than a script reading.

V95   When you're doing your research are you reaching out to people individually? Are you scraping the web for what's already there?

SWM   There is some scraping through the internet, but there are a lot of people that I'll talk to—without putting everyone's names out there.

V95   Sure.

SWM   But there are a lot of companies I'll talk to as well, based on what I'm going to go over, just to make sure everything is correct. Especially if there's a rumor going on with *Rumor Wave*, I'll talk to people... just to make sure there's at least some merit to what I'm talking about. People started noticing with *Rumor Wave* that a lot of the stuff ends up coming true, which is often because, for those videos anyway, I'll usually go out and ask around. But for *News Wave* it's a lot of pulling information together, reaching out to some people— you don't always hear back—and just trying to verify things through multiple sources. It kind of works out.

V95   I'm curious to zoom in on the Soulja Boy bubble

I THINK RIGHT NOW THE BIGGEST THING TO FOLLOW IS SERVICE-BASED CONTENT, BECAUSE EVERYBODY IS LOOKING AT STREAMING AS THE NEXT-GEN OF SYSTEMS.

Jon Downey, Spawn Wave Media

that you were really on top of while it was going on. Can you walk us through that story, for the record?

SWM Well, Soulja Boy decided to sell [a kind of knock-off] console which I had already seen before. It was a white XBox One-looking system. Before he even announced what he was doing I had thought about buying it for a tech *Tech Wave*. I had already seen the thing and I knew exactly what it was. So [when Soulja Boy announced] he was selling it I pulled it up on AliExpress and I filmed a video comparing [his and the original]. Next, I decided to order it from Amazon just for fun, because it was really cheap, and I also ordered it from Soulja Boy's website as well.

V95 Did you ever get it, by the way?

SWM No, but he did refund my money, I will say that. He never sent it. He didn't have any intention of sending it. I don't think anyone ever got that system, mostly because: as soon as he shipped it there would be some copyright issues. [Laughter.]

V95 Of course. Like the fact that nearly all of Nintendo's library came loaded on the system...

SWM Yeah. [Laughter.] Nintendo, Activision, UbiSoft. Everybody's stuff was on there. So somebody was going to come looking for him.

V95 What do you think he was up to? If he never intended to ship those systems, what do you think the game was?

SWM I think it was mostly for attention. I do know he's gone to some conventions like E3. I feel like he at least enjoys games but—

V95 I think he was trying to get into streaming too, right?

SWM   Yeah, he's into streaming, but for some reason his stream isn't great. It like runs at five frames per second or something weird. [Laughter.]

V95   Sure, sure. But anyway, these videos you made brought the channel a lot of attention, right?

SWM   Yes, the first Soulja Boy video I did, where I explained what he was selling and I showed where he was selling them from, I think that got about 1.3 million views.

V95   Do you have specific goals for growth? I mean, this started as a labor of love and turned into a business. Does the business have quantifiable metrics of where you'd like to be in a year? Two years?

SWM   I think one of the biggest things that YouTube creators fall into is the stats. A lot of people get either bummed out, depressed, or frustrated at times if there's a valley. You have peaks and valleys on YouTube all the time. One day you're not doing as well, but then the next day people are watching it, and you feel great. But basically

Video Games

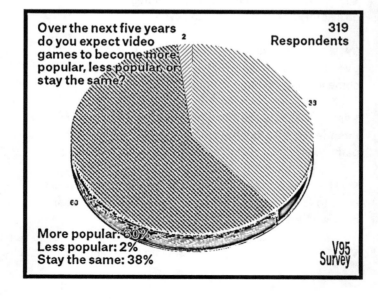

Over the next five years do you expect video games to become more popular, less popular, or stay the same?

319 Respondents

2

33

60

More popular: 60%
Less popular: 2%
Stay the same: 38%

V95 Survey

your sense of accomplishment is tied to YouTube and the stats that are in front of you when you log in. I guess [my first goal] was the same one that I think a lot of people have: 100,000 subscribers. [Because when you hit that number YouTube] sends you a special plaque so you have something you can hang up on the wall. At this point, for me, I think it's more or less just working towards having an actual office ... rather than just numbers. My next thought is to start getting to a point where I have an office and hire an editor so I can spend more time on things like *Tech Wave*. That's the goal now: hiring people and getting an actual space.

V95   It sounds like this is really a five- or ten-year goal, and this is really something you're working on for the foreseeable future. Is that correct?

SWM   Oh, yes. I've been around for a little over two years now, and you get thinking about that five-year, ten-year plan. There's still quite a ways to go, but I feel like I'm just getting started, so it's pretty cool.

V95   Looking to the future, then: we're at a moment where there's some speculation about the next gen being completely digital—or, at least, that we're not that far off from that... What do you see in the next five years of video game hardware and software? What are the big narratives for you to follow, looking to the future of video games?

SWM   I think right now the biggest thing to follow is service-based content, because everybody is looking at streaming as the next-gen of systems. I think the PlayStation 5 and the Xbox Scarlett, for example, will still have disc-based media; I don't think that's going to go away in the next gen. But I think the following gen, which would probably place us at nine or 10 years from now, will probably be disc-less. I think consoles are mostly going to become streaming devices, because they'll be cheaper. Google is getting ready to become part of the gaming scene, which is interesting.

V95   If the big three (Nintendo, Sony, and Microsoft) were to move away from making hardware and instead focus on developing streaming services, do you think we would start to see third-party hardware come out that provides a sort of universal console? A device that would allow you to switch back and forth between playing Nintendo, Sony, and Microsoft games? Kind of the way Apple TV is able to aggregate different content streaming services like Netflix, Hulu, etc.?

SWM   That's an interesting thought, to have one system. It's kind of a dangerous thought, too, to be honest—I'm not sure how that'd work with Nintendo or Sony, because they specifically sell systems to then sell their software. That's how they make a lot of their money...

V95   Nintendo especially has such a strong connection between hardware and software sales.

SWM   Yeah, Nintendo is an interesting company because they produce hardware that they make money on, which is weird. You don't usually see that. A lot of times a company will put out a system, lose money on it, and then make money back in the software. Sony, I think, broke that tradition with the PlayStation 4 and actually made a little bit of money on the PS4, even when it first came out. Nintendo generally makes $30 or $40 per each system they sell on launch day. They did that with the Switch. I don't think they would want to let go of their consoles right away...

V95   Changing the subject, I'm curious to know how you distinguish between work and play. When you're playing a game is your brain in work mode, or do you still relax with games?

SWM   Oh, that's actually a good question. That's the interesting thing—I used to work at all types of game stores, and then I ran one, and it did get to the point where I would go home and I wouldn't feel like playing games while

I was home. [Laughter.]

And I thought about that when I started with YouTube... I don't necessarily review games as much, so it helps that I'm talking more about the news cycle, and taking systems apart and stuff. I do know people who review stuff, and when they review a game they generally will sit down and play for, like, 15 hours at a time. I would be concerned about getting burned out from games at that point, but a couple of them do set aside time to just play a game that they're not reviewing and just have fun with it.

V95   How many hours a week would you say that you work?

SWM   Let's see... About 50 hours. 50 hours a week.

V95   You're working by yourself—you do have family around— does it ever get lonely? I watch the *SpawnCast* when you stream it live on YouTube and everyone seems to have a great time hanging out online, talking about the news. Do you ever hang out with those guys in person?

SWM   Yeah, I'll got to a lot of [gaming] events throughout the year and usually I'll see a lot of different YouTube personalities at those. But generally, I'm actually fine spending time at home by myself, and exercising at the gym pretty much every day. I don't mind some of the solitude, it's actually nice, believe it or not. With getting a little older it's actually nice. The solitude's good. [Laughter.]

V95   Anything else you'd like to add that I've missed?

SWM   I think that's... Well, we do all have to pay taxes, so it's technically a real job. [Laughter.]

V95   Is it freelancer's tax?

SWM   A 1099, yeah. People would be a bit surprised at how much—that was just on my mind because we were filing them, so... [Laughter.] I know people don't see it as a real job, but the IRS sees it differently, so... [Laughter.]

V95   Sure. And, they're kind of the ones that matter.

SWM   Yep, those YouTubers pay quite a bit in taxes.

V95   OK, one more question then. How do you feel about YouTube's monetization policies, and them as a sort of parent company generally? Do you think they're fair?

SWM   Me, yes. I actually have an easy relationship with YouTube. There are things I adopted on my channel after I did a lot of research on the monetization policies. For example, I don't actually curse on my channel at all.

V95   No, I noticed. Yeah.

SWM   And that's on purpose—sometimes I'll get emails from parents who say that they are happy to put me on the TV for their kids because they don't have to worry about that. And I like that because it means that my son can watch it sooner than later, when he gets old enough. I pretty much just keep it all gaming-related, and don't try to get too much into the politics of the games or anything. And it helps. I've always been fine with YouTube, but I probably have a different viewpoint [about how monetization works] than people who "hit the hornet's nest" at times...

V95   Do you communicate with YouTube at all? Asking questions or offering ideas?

SWM   Oh, no, there is no real communication between creators and YouTube. Usually we have to figure things out on the fly. If an algorithm changes, we have to figure out, "Okay, is it this a tag? Or, does my thumbnail need to be changed? Or, does...?" We've gotten to the point where our titles have to be semi-bombastic—you see it all over YouTube. Generally, you have to have a thumbnail that has a weird face, or a picture of you in it or something, to help the algorithms. Unfortunately, they don't tell us [how the algorithms work]. And I think they don't tell us because they don't want people to manipulate the way it all works, and I get that...

V95   Well, thanks for bringing up your taxes so we could get a little bit more of that back-end info.

SWM   Oh, sure. I know a lot of YouTubers don't talk about it. And a lot of people just assume that YouTubers don't pay taxes. But, no: we actually pay a lot of taxes. [Laughter.]

Videogames will still be a way of escaping reality and having fun (-with friends). They might become more integrated in our daily lifes like school for example.

I hope until then we have achieved a complete augmented reality as part of playing video games so you yourself can enter the world of gaming A substitute for friends/family for lonely people, a way to kill some time for "normal" people. Maybe. I don't really know.

They will obviously improve over time but video games brought us closer. We all have something to play and talk about.

I feel it will be a form of bonding with family's. The same way it was with TV in the years prior.

If we're still around, I believe video games will have a huge cultural impact that'll affect our daily lives in ways we can't imagine. I'd imagine virtual reality would be huge thing and nearly inescapable. That, or video games will be a complete relic of the past entirely

Video Games are my greatest passion and guide me through life.

It might be a new way to communicate, or make friends

People could become entirely detached from reality while living in the digital. I wouldn't be surprised if we reach Sword Art Online levels of immersion in the next 20 years.

Schools could use AR or VR for learning and they could be more integrated such as pokemon go and shit

i feel the world will be artificial. everything, everyone will be a game.

I think that video games will be something that people will look up to. Or something like that.

Stress relief, recreational activities, or full time/part time jobs. Streaming will become more predominant, as well as Esports.

In the 80s-90s, video games had many innovations and the goal from companies seemed to be "stand out." Nowadays, the motto seems to be "cash out" only innovating ways of profiting, rather than the landscape of the gaming world. I feel as if videogames will be somewhat less popular in 2069 and many more alternatives will be available.

So long as they're not laden with MTX, they should be amazing.

Form of expression

It will be a job.

I think video games will be the most accessible, timeless and popular form of art by the time 2069 (nice) rolls around.

It will become a very common leisurely activity that will bleed into the competitive realm like sports. It will become an incredible social platform that offers virtual interaction between people across the world. Which is basically how it is now, but think of that ×1000

Video games will be played across the board by all ages. People in their 60-80s will play just as much as they would in present day. Gen X and beyond grew up with this entertainment and it will be a universal form of entertainment from kids to seniors.

I think games will only become immersive over time, such that the boundaries between elements of a gaming experience and even trivial details of one's daily existence may become difficult to tell apart.

maybe a way to escape the wasteland of a destroyed earth or just a pass time

Better hand eye coordination, reflexes etc

I don't think I can think so I don't answer

Although I don't think video games could be apart of everyone's daily life, I 100% believe they will be more widespread than ever, and possibly even the most dominant form of media worldwide.

They will be used to tell a story in a more immersive way (with vr, for example)

A simulation for both the lonely and otherwise.

I think it will be like Ready Player One.

the same role that we find today, but greater possibilities to become something serious as a sport.

It's possible some other form of entertainment will rise up by then. Video games haven't been accessible to the public for 60 years and there's been lots of change within its lifespan, so I doubt people will be focused on the next console or the hot new game of the month / year in that time.

Ready Player One without the dystopian part.

Video games will continue to be our escape from reality. When the real world becomes to much to bare, we can find solace in virtual worlds that continue to present settings that tend to be dynamically more unqiue than what most of us are able to experience on Earth. Not everyone has the privilege or resources to experience the unfamiliar in this world, so they make up for it by substituting reality with a fabricated one. There are also cases where some adventures can only ever be experienced in the world of a game.

VR will take over, TV will fade and On demmand film scriveces like Netflix/Hulu and videogames will replace Television. People won't think of videogames as a hobby anymore, people will think about videogames like we think of TV.

I guess they Will be a way tô socialise. They Will be like social medias and Second Life.

Video games will continue to tell stories too unconventional for film and other mediums, and will also likely replace experiences in real life.

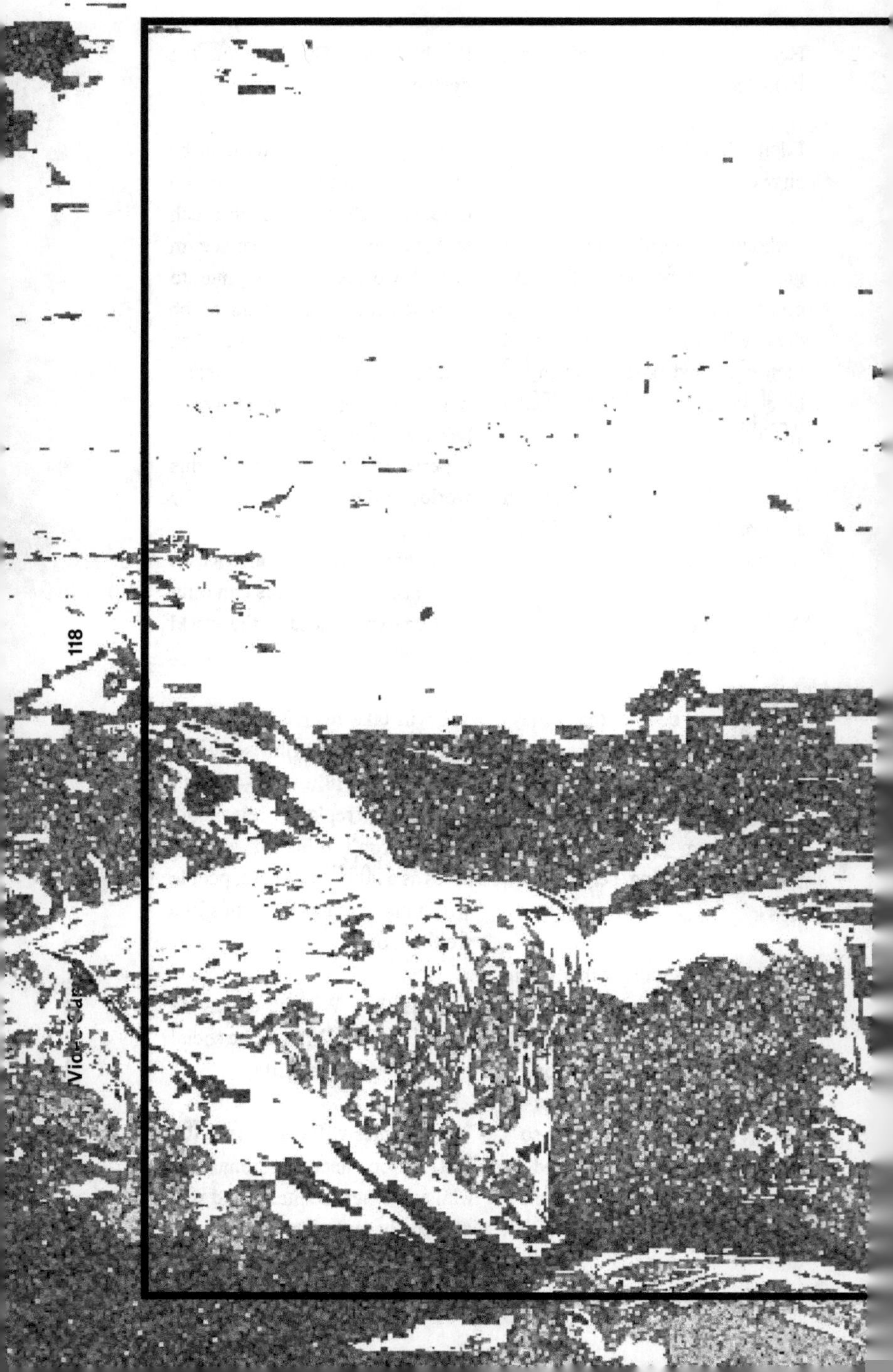

Commonwealth
Realm

Konrad Vaernes + Joseph Ferris

V95   How'd Commonwealth Realm get going?

K   Taking the plunge into this was completely spontaneous—It felt like I lost control of myself a little bit when I uploaded those few first videos. It was just like, "Okay. This is amazing." I was just doing it without thinking about what I was doing. And then one of those videos started getting a good number of views, like thirty or forty thousand, and when that's one of your first videos, you start thinking, "Okay. Maybe this is something."

     I was in Portugal [at the time] and didn't have much to do except go to the beach—so I just sat in a time-share condo and worked on *Zelda* [videos]. In many ways [*Zelda*] was the series the channel ran on until E3 2015, when I started expanding a little bit, getting more into the Switch rumors. I was also trying out different timeline [videos] as well. First with a few *Zelda* subjects, like the Zora timeline and Sheikah timeline. I think I met Joseph—was it E3 2015?

J   Well, I remember we did our first collaboration when I had my separate channel—I still have my separate channel—after the 2015 Game Awards. Because there was no *Zelda* [announcement] and we were wondering what the hell was going on. And then later on you asked me to join the channel right before E3 2016 because we knew that was going to be the big reveal [of the next *Zelda*].

K   Yeah, I thought it would be beneficial to team up... We did few other videos as well. But for some reason they didn't perform so well. Back then I had absolutely no knowledge of how YouTube channels really work. I was just doing my thing. I was getting lucky mostly because of collaborations. Without the collaborations I've done, especially early on, I don't think the channel would be where it is now. Back then, what can I say... I was ashamed of my Norwegian accent, because I'm not a native English speaker. I thought the videos would just get better if I also had some native English speakers from the UK, US or Canada. And so I was looking for collaborators.

In many ways, those different collaborations were what got me to the first ten thousand subscribers. When we teamed up with Joseph in May 2016, I think the channel had around fifteen thousand subscribers.

V95   Was there a specific moment when you decided to monetize?

K   I'll be completely honest, for about the first three months, I didn't know you could make money on YouTube. I didn't really think much about it until Joseph came on and I had to think about paying him and, later on, our editors. It didn't matter that much to me before that point.

V95   Anything to add to the origin story, Joseph? Maybe a little bit of your own background too?

J   Totally. So I have this other YouTube channel, Ferris Wheel Productions, because my last name is Ferris. And by the time this book comes out, it's probably going to be called FerrisWheelPro. I was just doing video game reviews, but I wanted to make them kind of like Angry Video Game Nerd, JonTron, and all those YouTubers who incorporate live-action comedic sketches into their stuff. After I joined [Commonwealth Realm] I didn't pay that much attention to my other channel. But now now I'm starting to build a following on that channel again.

Working on Commonwealth Realm is interesting. When I started I had a part-time job at movie theatres. It was always a struggle to find the time to edit. Many late nights... But when we started making some serious dough through YouTube and Patreon I decided it was time to quit the stupid movie theatre job. And granted, I still work a part-time job over the weekends because it's a guaranteed, consistent paycheck. YouTube's unpredictable in that regard. But as a job: I get to talk about video games, edit a lot of footage of video games, and sometimes even play video games for most of the week. It's a blessing, truly.

V95   What's your normal working process like?

K   We sit down and write a script, and then try to match footage with whatever we are saying. That's pretty much what we do. It sounds *much* easier than it is.

V95   I'm sure!

K   That's one thing that many people underestimate. They think, "Oh, you just write your thoughts and make a video." But when you are talking about ten different games and you need footage for all of them finding and editing that footage becomes very time-consuming.

V95   How do you divide the work between the two of you? Given how far apart you live from one another [Norway and California], how do you work around the time difference?

K   We have learned to know when the other person is awake [Laughter], let's just put it that way. My schedule is kind of a mess at times. For the most part, Joey doesn't edit anything on weekends when he's doing his other job, so I usually take care of operations on weekends. And we try to make sure that we don't edit more than one video per week—there are exceptions, of course, like if a Nintendo Direct happens—but otherwise, we try to make sure that we're not overworked. And we try to have as much transparency as possible between us when it comes to workload. A key part of why we're not really tired of this is that we are able to say when we can work and when we cannot.

J   Yeah, and it helps when you we have a crew of people. We have two other editors that help out occasionally, and they're ridiculously talented, so without them we'd go crazy.

V95   Right, and you occasionally hire the same voice actor, correct?

J   Yes, Jason Damron. And coincidentally, [Jason and I] live in the same city, pretty much— same county... So that was kind of funny because Konrad hired Jason way before he hired me. [Laughter] It's a small world we live in...

K   Yeah, I was just shocked. I can visit Joseph and visit Jason at the same time, which is exactly what I've done. Our biggest challenge has always been making live-action content when we are so far away from each other. It's pretty much half the globe.

V95   Could you walk me through your setup? What kind of technology have you decided you need in order to make the kind of content you want to make?

K   Well, it's mostly editing programs. Microphones, a camera with a microphone, and a capture card, of course.

J   Yeah, we both have Canon DSLRs. I have a Rebel T3i that I've been using for years. You're using a 60D now, right, buddy?

K   No, 70D.

J   70D, yeah. We also got green screens from Elgato and have used those a couple of times... Sometimes when I'm doing a simple live-action intro, I just set up one light and talk to my webcam. But if I'm already filming something for my other channel and I still need to film live-action for Commonwealth Realm, I'll just knock that out because my camera equipment, the green screen, and the lights are already up.

V95   Sure.

K   We also Elgato capture cards, but I just switched AVerMedia because I have a 4K TV.

J   Yeah, I've also been thinking about changing capture cards because Elgato has had some issues as of late... And that card is three years old at this point?

K   Yeah.

J   So it starts to show. Sometimes when you're recording it starts skipping, which is very annoying. [Laughter.]

V95   After the video is up, do you share the work of assessing how the video is performing? What constitutes good performance for you?

K   One of the biggest struggles has been to keep a consistent viewer base on each video. There has been quite a variety over the years. But the thing is—we also talked about this with our network manager—our channel is very robust when it comes to long-term [viewership]. We're not a fluke. We have been here for years and our views are rather stable. We average a little below one hundred thousand per video... And that's absolutely acceptable. Of course, my long-term goal is to have an average of over one hundred thousand per video. But that requires some equipment that I don't have right now, as well as changing the format a little bit.

V95   Do you keep up with the comments?

K   Oh, absolutely. I try to comment on every video that we upload, at least for the first few hours, because after that you just completely lose track and need to move to another project.

The Pokémon Timeline (With Sun and Moon) - Ft Gnoggin

2.9M views · 2 years ago

Legend of Zelda Timeline (With Breath of the Wild)

2M views · 2 years ago

Top 10 Nintendo Switch Games!

1.5M views · 5 months ago

Top 10 Upcoming Nintendo Switch Games in 2019-2020!

1M views · 4 months ago

Zelda Theory: Zora Timeline and History

539K views · 1 year ago

Zelda Theory: The Complete Legend of Zelda Timeline...

529K views · 3 years ago

Best Nintendo Switch Accessories in 2018

715K views · 10 months ago

Nintendo Switch E3 2019 Games!

573K views · 3 weeks ago

V95   How do you pick what you cover in your videos?

K   Sometimes [choosing] what to cover can be rather challenging. When you don't do news videos, you are kind of bound to specific games and topics. We have to make up our own topics and think, "Will this be something that our viewers want to watch?" And that's the biggest challenge of it all. Sometimes you have no idea if it will perform or not. A perfect example of that was when we did "Nintendo Switch Accessories"—I think it was last year, shortly after E3—and we had no idea how well that video would do. It currently sits, I think, at around six hundred thousand views or something.

J   That was shocking.

K   And it's just like, you have no idea. You go back a few months later and find out—"Wow, did this video do *that* well?" The same goes with "Top 10 Nintendo Switch Games" that we did back in December. Now it sits at seven hundred thousand views, and I'm just like, "Why can't all the videos perform like this?" [Laughter.] Sometimes it's just the perfect timing, it's the perfect video for that time of the year. We all know that Christmas videos tend to perform better. And yeah, people tend to watch the big production [videos] a bit more, but those are weeks and weeks of work and sometimes you ask yourself, "Was this worth it?" Because when you have to put so much effort into one video, the salary per hour is not good. [Laughter.] It's rather terrible.

V95   Do you feel that the YouTube monetization policy is fair?

K   I will say that it's better than it used to be. The thing about ad revenue is that it fluctuates. There are some months when you do better, and the later half of the year is obviously better, with Christmas. But then there are months where you are barely able to make a living... I live in Norway, which is one of the most expensive countries in the world, and I'm making a living off YouTube. It's nearly impossible. [Laughter.]

V95   For sure.

J   I would say months like January just suck.

V95   Sure. Christmas is over, there's nothing really going on in the news cycle.

J   Exactly. Don't even bother uploading in January... [Laughter.]

K   Yeah, we always think we need to feed the algorithm, but you never know what it wants. That's the big challenge: you never know how well a video will do until it's been up for, say, a week or so. And sometimes it takes even longer than that. We have seen videos that we thought were complete flops suddenly make a surge—a perfect example was the *Spider-Man* review last year, Joey.

J   That video was sitting at like 5,500 views for a week. But then, all of a sudden, the next Saturday it shot up to like 60,000, and we were like, "Okay, what?" [Laughter.]

V95   Do you have a sense of why that happened?

J   I guess more people started beating *Spider-Man* and they wanted to look at more videos about it? [Laughter.] I don't know, maybe some big person shared it.

K   Another thing I also want to get back to is that there are different types of content, which is important for people who want to start up in YouTube to learn about. You have short time videos, which are typical news videos, and then there reviews and comparison videos—

J   Or the timelines

Look at Nintendo Switch

Nintendo NX

K —those are things that people are willing to watch for months or years to come. So one of the main priorities I set for this channel was that we didn't want to have short-term content. Because feeding the algorithm every single day would break us, it would simply break us as human beings and creators.

J And sometimes the algorithm punishes you for uploading every day.

K It buries you.

J Yeah, because subscribers aren't willing to watch that many videos.

K They're not. Exactly.

V95 Right, right. It's sort of limited, everybody has a limited attention that they spread, probably between you and the several other channels.

K J Exactly.

K You can imagine having a mental breakdown needing to upload a video every day. In fact, I had a mental breakdown last year, and what saved the channel was that I had Joseph, and I other editors. I was able to focus on just writing and recording until I was able to pick myself up again and start making solid content.

V95 Definitely. It sounds like A) you're obviously not a fluke, and B) you think carefully about sustainability. Is this something that you see yourself doing in one year? In five years? What does that future look like for both of you?

J That's a good question... Maybe one of these days I'll say, "I did what I want with YouTube. It's time for me to just relax, get a regular job, and just play games for fun." [Laughter.] That's just my thing. But as of right now, I'm still riding on that YouTube train. I don't know when I'm going to stop.

K   I see this as, pretty much, my foreseeable future. The thing is, making Nintendo [related] content is something you will be able to do for a long time to come, but when it comes to YouTube as a platform, that's something I'm a little more uncertain about.

      The thing about Nintendo is that it's a rather predictable company in term of their IPs. There's a cycle. There's a *Zelda* cycle, there's a Mario cycle, there's a Smash cycle... And because of that, you always have something new to talk about. Because Nintendo has been around for 130 years, they're experts. And besides, they have such big [cash] reserves that I see them making games for the next thirty, forty, maybe even fifty years. This company is just what defines "video game." If you ask people what video games are, the probability is very high that they will say Nintendo or *Mario* or *Pokemon* or Pikachu or whatever.

      But with YouTube, I think we will one day see a competent competitor come out. And hopefully they will be better, both revenue-wise and copyright-wise.

V95   You're in communication online, but is it important that you guys do meet in person once or twice a year? Does it ever get lonely working by yourselves?

J   I think it is important that we meet in person once or twice every year, which we've been pretty consistent about these past two years. It remind us who we're working with, and how the other person works. Because there's only so much that goes through Skype, Google Hangouts, Facebook Messenger, all that stuff. As for lonely work, I mean, it depends on who you are as a person. If you're an extrovert, this is going to be super lonely for you, let's be honest.

K   Okay, I just have to say it. Being a Nintendo YouTuber in Norway is lonely. Very, very lonely. I guess that's why I'm so active in the comment sections and why I try to speak with the community, because I just feel I have no community of my own here in Norway.

V95   And your fans appreciate the communication, I'm sure.

J   It's good to communicate with your fans, no matter how big you are—just don't go and reply to every single comment because that would kill you. Although that's what I'm doing on my other channel because I don't get that many comments. Right now I'm watching a bunch of videos that are basically YouTube how-tos... how to get more viewers, get more subscribers... And it's all about engagement, it's all about looking at your statistics. It's all about figuring out what works. All that good stuff.

K   Yeah, and we also try to meet face-to-face with the community and the industry, going to E3 or PACs and so on.

V95   Are you friends with any of the other YouTubers who run gaming related channels?

K   It's one thing to have friends in the YouTube community, but it's also about having a little bit of a rivalry. It just pushes you to do better. And overall it's just a good thing, because you realize, "Okay, there's where we can improve," and see your own mistakes from a whole new light and perspective.

J   A lot of our Nintendo community friends are in New York, which is why we go there, as well. You go to [the Nintendo] store and the line is full of all of the fricken Nintendo YouTubers we know.

V95   Are you in communication with Nintendo? Do they send you advance copies of games?

J   They don't send us advanced copies anymore.

They just stopped doing that... Apparently, some Nintendo Ambassador leaked a game early, and it was a big game, so as a result most of us Nintendo Ambassadors got punished for it.

V95   Do you think it's fair to say that the Nintendo fan base is a bit more fanatical about Nintendo's IPs than maybe Sony or Microsoft fans are about their first party exclusives?

K   I don't know. I don't want to mischaracterize the other two as having lackluster fan bases, but I find that when I'm going on a general YouTube hunt of channels that are specific to software, I find a lot more for Nintendo.

J   Yeah, there are these websites called "enthusiast" websites. There's Nintendo Enthusiast, PlayStation Enthu-

I believe that there will be a much more inclusive way to play video games than today. I think that VR is going to advance and become a way for people to escape reality even more. Not to get too Black Mirror-ish and futuristic but technology advances fast and the reason we love video games is because we're controlling something else and doing amazing things. If technology moves towards making the way you play more like YOU are in the game, then I think the market can only grow. 2069 is 50 years away. Look how far video games have come in 50 years. Just my take on it. Hope I could help! Love the page.

vr will become so emersive that people will start to hang out whit friends in vr. This will be seen as a normal thing.

I think video games will be very prominent and everywhere and it will be a lot more accessible through things like VR and even mixed with our own reality

In 2069 life itself will be a video game.

Entertainment

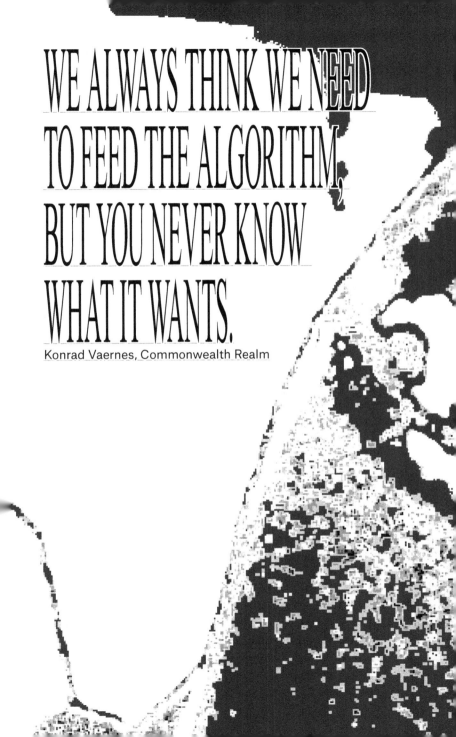

WE ALWAYS THINK WE NEED TO FEED THE ALGORITHM, BUT YOU NEVER KNOW WHAT IT WANTS.

Konrad Vaernes, Commonwealth Realm

siast, and Xbox Enthusiast. The most active one is Nintendo Enthusiast by a huge mile. I would say the Nintendo fan base is bigger and more passionate, but I can't really say that definitively because I surround myself with those kind of people.

V95   Konrad, anything to add there?

K   Nintendo is Nintendo. It's pretty much the Disney of the video game world. And their IPs are more or less timeless: *Mario*, *Zelda*, *Smash* and even the likes of *Metroid*. It's that simple. Because Nintendo is very orthodox and traditional in their approach to games. Actually, I would say they fit the definition of conservatism very well. That is, they change to maintain. That's what their big strength is. No *Mario* game is identical. *Zelda* is a different game every time, and you get shocked by the art style, the direction of gameplay, the setting, and so on. And the fact that Nintendo is able to reinvent themselves within those set boundaries, and within those IPs, is what keeps them so in touch with the rest of the video game world. They know what works, and they know what to do in order to keep that working for the foreseeable future.

V95   Do you see them continuing to avoid microtransactions?

J   I see them avoiding that for a long time—maybe not permanently, but they haven't fallen into that trap yet. We're not seeing any microtransactions in Splatoon, which is their biggest online shooter. I hope we don't see any in *Metroid Prime 4*, which has an online shooting mechanic. We'll see.

K   The main reason I don't think we'll see anything like [microtransactions] is because Nintendo is a much more kid-focused developer and publisher. And, as we all know, loot boxes and microtransactions have some connections to gambling. I think that Nintendo is well aware of that. And besides, there's a completely different culture in Japan when it comes to gambling and how you sell extras to your product. Again, Nintendo is very traditional. And that's what people appreciate about them: they are not here to make a half-finished product and then sell the rest of it to you in chunks.

V95   What advice would you give to anyone looking to get into making videos for YouTube?

K   ...You need to be passionate about what you do, you need to be consistent, and you need a few partners to work with. If you do this alone, sooner or later you will burn out.

J   Yeah, but the thing is: everyone that goes into You-Tube has a different starting point and wants to do different things. So it's not simple.

K   My advice would be: if you're trying to make gaming or Nintendo content on YouTube, don't start covering just news. Why would people want to watch you when they can watch everyone else cover the news? You need to do something that stands out, and most importantly, you need to be consistent. Starting with at least one video per week. You shouldn't burn yourself out already if you're not getting paid to do it... You've got to figure out what your niche is and how to stand out.

J   Yeah. That, and making good thumbnails is key.

V95   The thumbnails help feed the algorithm, right?

J   Oh yeah... [Laughter.]

How much do you agree or disagree with the following statement: "Some video games are works of art."

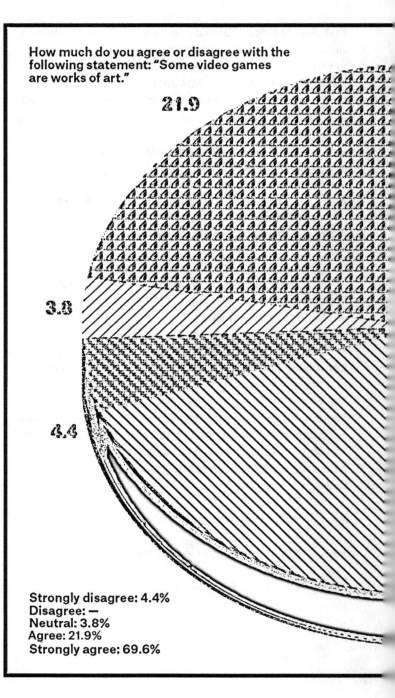

21.9

3.8

4.4

Strongly disagree: 4.4%
Disagree: —
Neutral: 3.8%
Agree: 21.9%
Strongly agree: 69.6%

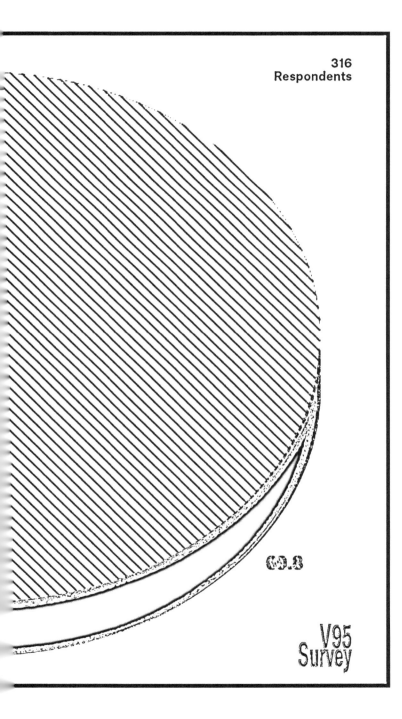

316
Respondents

69.8

V95
Survey

Maynarde

Leigh Mandalov

SELECT

V95   How would you describe the work that you do?

M   That's been a bit tough. In Australia, specifically
in [part of the country] I live in, not a whole lot of people
do what I do. But I describe myself as an online broadcast
personality or a commentator. Usually what follows when
I'm speaking to your regular Joe here in South Australia is,
"What does that mean?" And I'll just say, "You know how
football has commentators? I'm one of those but for video
games." And then they'll usually go, "Oh, [lightbulb] Okay.
All right. Now I get it." The next question is always, "Is
there money in that?" And I'll say, "Well, it's enough to live
by at the moment." And they're always surprised. That's
something I go through every time I go to a dinner party or
a house party of some kind. And I'm a streamer as well, but
explaining "streamer" to people is also a bit tough.

V95   Right, when you're out at a party with 'regular joes'
and whatnot.

M   Yeah, with a bunch of what we would call normies.
[Laughter.] Regular Joes. Regular people.

V95   Are you working exclusively with *StarCraft II*? Walk
us through a bit of your career trajectory as a commentator.

M   I don't really cast anything other than *StarCraft II*.
I do stream other games from time to time on my Twitch
channel, but as far as being a part of a live show—wearing a
full suit and a headset, standing at the desk—I've only ever
casted the *Overwatch* launch event in Australia. I was the
host for that. And one other time [Zepph], who's another

Australian commentator, she and I dabbled in running a local *Overwatch* league. Not The *Overwatch* League, because that's a big thing, but a local *Overwatch* tournament. We thought it was really fun, but it was also very hard to commentate. [Zepph] and I are really excited about the game. And I think the commentators of The *Overwatch* League do a great job with it, but maybe their eyes and brain process things faster than mine do, I don't know! [laughter] It just seems so hard to follow.

V95   I agree.

M   There are 12 players, they have all 'ultimates', they're all switching characters live, on the fly... It's impossible to cover it all, whereas in *StarCraft* you'll miss something every now and then but it's all there. You can see it all. You have a top-down view of it, literally. And things like a production tab and whatnot [to monitor the game in other ways]. It just feels like a really natural eSport. And then, within *StarCraft*, 99.99% of what I've done has been *StarCraft II*. I have done a couple casts of *StarCraft I*, but only on my stream and nothing in any official capacity with Blizzard or with any kind of big tournament. But with *StarCraft II*, I've done a lot, with Blizzard, IEM, DreamHack—everyone.

V95   What was your first experience as a professional commentator like?

M   "Starting in commentating" is a story that I've told a few times just to people in chat—I get that question a lot when I stream. "How did you get into commentating? How did you get where you are?" I was really, really into *StarCraft II* as soon as it got released. I was really, really hyped for it to be released. I remember sitting my girlfriend down to watch each new release trailer whenever they came out. I was just so excited. I had a friend give me his Battlenet so I could play the beta. And then when it came out I hit the game really hard. I jumped into the the local community, and started signing up for local tournaments and local clan leagues. I was really into the clan league that we had at the time, which was for lower levels. I was playing in it, but I got eliminated pretty quickly because I was never—and I'm still not—very good. So one night I was having a few drinks watching people play and enjoying myself when the guy that was casting announced: "Well, my co-caster's cancelled on me. So anyone who adds me on Skype, first come, first served: you can co-cast with me." I was sipping on my whiskey and I was like, "Yeah. sure. I'll do that. Why not?" I added him on Skype and that was that...

And then, later, one of the guys that was running a more official league in the region invited me to co-cast a cup he was running. And he guy ended up being the go-to for ACL [Australian Cyber League], which would eventually become ESL Australia, and who now run IEM Sydney... and so on and so on. That was that: I was in the international circuit. It was just a word-of-mouth thing, a who-you-know thing. But I also like to think that I'm alright at it. That first cast people basically said, "Oh, he's got a nice voice. He's funny. He's making jokes. We like him."

V95   Have you been actively thinking about how you develop your persona as a caster? You're an amazing hype man. Are you actually, authentically hyped when you cast?

M   I've very rarely sat down and thought, "I should do more of this or that when I cast." Feedback can be tricky. Some people don't want to tell you what you did wrong. And some people just don't know what you did wrong. So it's really good to get feedback from your fellow commentators. Or sometimes my wife, who listens to me a lot at home, will give me feedback. But as far as the hype goes, I'm just really naturally excited. It's not fake. And it really bothers me when people call [my excitement] fake. People have called me all kinds of weird things, but whenever they call me fake, it's really annoying because I'm not that. I can't actually fake it. That's part of the reason why I haven't done other eSports. Other games have tried to offer me

casting jobs over the years. I think what they want that excitement, that hype. But I don't think I can do that naturally, organically with other games because I'm not excited by them.

V95 The casting community of *StarCraft II* seems really tight knit. I see online that you all hang out socially around events. Have you ever considered moving to be closer to your fellow casters in the States or Europe?

M Yeah. We hang out. But it's tough because we all live in different parts of the world. For me, getting anywhere is a long trip and it's expensive. Whenever the Europeans travel to America or vice versa they always meet up with each other and catch up. They hang out and have dinner, or spend a day going to the casino together or something like that. I would do the same if the guys lived anywhere near me because we are really good friends. I think that comes through in the broadcast as well. We're at worst friends and at best very good friends. We talk to each other a lot through social networks, like Twitter and Discord. And whenever we're streaming, at least a few of those personalities will be in the chat.

It's not a physical thing. We're not in the same space very often, which would be nice. From time to time, find myself thinking, "Oh, geez, I wish I had someone to hang out with today." But the reason why I don't move is because I have a really good living situation: I have a house and I live here with a wife, and I don't want my wife to give up her life here just to follow me somewhere. I have a dog. I like where I live. The pros of moving don't outweigh the pros of staying, for me. I would rather put up with the brutal travel and come home to where I live than move internationally. I already took a huge risk leaving my full-time job to do this full-time, and taking another huge risk like that I think is a bit too risky.

Considering the climate of *StarCraft II* and eSports... It's been growing very organically over the last couple years, which is wonderful, but there've been some big things happening internationally that [can be troubling]. Like all those layoffs at Blizzard, for example. Who's to say that one day Blizzard doesn't just axe WCS? If that happens my safety net would be pulled out from under me. I mean, that's terrifying to think about.

V95   What do you think would happen if Blizzard suddenly decided to shut down WCS?

M   Well, the only thing that Blizzard can shut down is WCS, because they control that. But there are definitely other community tournaments and events that are run by people other than Blizzard. WSG is not Blizzard. HomeStory Cup is a big tournament, that's not Blizzard. But if WCS went away, people would be less excited about the game, and the good momentum that the game has right now would cease. I do think that people will continue to play the game, and I do think that people will continue their own tournaments. But, if Blizzard pulled the plug I don't think there would be enough money to sustain most of the professional players and casters. I think a lot of that would go away, unfortunately.

V95   There has been, for a long time, the narrative of "Korea versus the rest of the world" in *StarCraft II*. Could you talk a bit about where that comes from or what maintains that divide between the levels of Korean play and non-Korean play?

M   I think a lot of the reason why Korea is "better" is because the *StarCraft II* scene has been a big part of the country's eSport history for 20 years. Korea was the first place to really make *Brood War* explode, and it was the first place to have big companies invest in actual, professional teams that were run by actual coaches, ex-pro gamers and that sort of thing. They would basically run these teams like sweatshops, where they would practice against each other 14 hours a day and only take breaks to sleep and eat a little. When *StarCraft II* was released, it was a similar story where big teams—big brands, rather, like telecommunication companies and airlines were picking up teams and paying salaries for these kids to do nothing but play the game all day, every day. Whereas internationally, in the Western world, while some of those teams did exist, the people on those teams wouldn't practice as hard. There are some people that would put in similar amounts of work, but the big international teams like, say, your Team Liquids, your Evil Geniuses, had a *StarCraft II* team. You could tell they were maybe a bit more of a frat house? [Laughter.] They were practicing, but nowhere near as much as the Koreans. [For the Korean teams] being good is their *life*. It's a grind for them, doing nothing but playing the game all day. I'm sure that they still enjoy themselves on some level. But they have those work regiments in their brain.

V95   How many hours a week would you say you're working, including streaming and everything? You said that you've left a full-time job to pursue this work. Does your week have kind of a rhythm? Do you schedule your stream? How rigorous are you with that sort of thing?

M   At the moment, the only thing that's scheduled for me to do every week Tuesday night when I cast Oli-moLeague, which is the biggest online Korean *StarCraft II* league. I'm the English stream for that and have been for

the last six months or so.

That's been my baby and that's pretty big for the channel, but as far as my personal streams go, I usually do between four to six hours each day. I take weekends off because that's when my wife's not working and we'll hang out. I like spending time with her, and I want to make sure that we spend time together. Monday to Friday I'll stream every day, and when I'm not doing that I'll be doing something related to my stream for another two hours a day, thereabouts. For instance, I usually have commentary or replay casts and that sort of thing, and then I'll have to do a bunch of preparation to make sure that I'm ready for the next stream. Some days I'll stream way more than that. For instance, on Tuesday when I stream the tournament, I'll stream for four to six hours like I regularly would, take a three hour break and then commentate the tournament for another four to six hours.

V95   Does it ever wear you down? Do you feel like you have a good sense of time management?

M   Sometimes I wish I could manage myself a bit better. But I'd say nine times out of ten, I've got a good handle on things. I've got a good rhythm going on, and I like it quite a bit. I always told myself that if I'm going to leave my full-time job I'm still going to put full-time hours. Because it is really one of those things where you get what you put into it, for the most part. Especially when you're at the level I am. I'm not trying to break into the scene, and I'm not trying to grow a channel from scratch. I got partnered quickly because people at Twitch knew who I was. Things like Twitch partnership and having a following came really quickly because I was already an international commentator. I had a big leg up when I started streaming. So for me, the more hours I put in, the more subscribers and followers I get.

And when I go away, for instance, when I go away to IEM and I don't stream for a week my Twitch progress evaporates. I happens so quickly, like scarily fast. When I'm

Leigh "Maynarde" Mandalov

gone for a week, I'll actually lose close to 30% of my sub-scribers. The reason why that happens is because Twitch, at the moment, has things like Twitch Prime, which resets every month. There's also sub gifting, where someone will gift you 20 subs and then after a month those subs go away unless they renew themselves manually, which is very rare.

V95   Do you think in terms of a five-year, ten-year plan for growth with your Twitch specifically, or with your career in general? Where do you see yourself in that kind of a timeframe?

M   I'm a big believer in the universe [and the fact that] there are going to be a lot of things you can't control. It's not about what you deserve and it's not about what you think is fair. You should concentrate on what you can control: and that's where I'm at. I'm just trying to make sure that I'm doing the best with what I can control. I hope the game continues to grow, which is the case at the moment. We're on that trajectory. And I do hope that in five years time I'm still doing what I'm doing right now, because I don't really want to do anything else. The idea of doing something else actually depresses me [laughter]. I want to always be happy with my career and with what I do. And I want the effort I put into my career to equate to greater results.

That's the great thing about being a Twitch streamer: it's kind of like entrepreneurship. Your channel is your own company and you can decide how to use your resources to make improvements.

V95   What kind of equipment have you invested in to grow the channel?

M   A lot of people have told me I have a great voice. So I have the best microphone and audio equipment money can buy. I've also gotten better webcams and better PCs so that my stream is high-quality. I do all my graphics work myself. I put in a lot of work to make [the stream] a good product.

V95   How would you recommend a newbie go about assembling their streaming setup?

M   First I would recommend that they have a system with a good enough CPU and video card to be able to stream at least 720p at 60 FPS. Basically, at the minimum, you need to be able to play the games you want to stream at a decent quality. You don't need to be a 1080p, high-encoding whatever. You don't need to have the greatest looking stream on Twitch, you just need to have a stream that is sort of up to 2019 quality, which I think is at minimum 720p with 60 frames per second. That, and people undervalue how important microphone and audio quality is. You don't need the most expensive mic. You can get a really good dynamic mic for not that much.

Next, make sure that you're comfortable because you're going to want to put in hours. You can't stream three hours, three times a week and expect your stream to grow, especially if you're just starting. Like I mentioned, I had a leg up, but even so, I am still one of the smallest streams in *StarCraft II* compared to my caster brothers and sisters. My stream is a fraction of people like iNcontroL, and RotterdaM. If you're starting from absolutely nothing, you need to put in some serious hours and you need to be consistent. You need to be live every single day and doing six to eight hours (at least, I would say) every single day. And don't be afraid to use social networking, to message personalities, people that have a following, and be like, "Hey, man. I'm a fan. I love your stuff. And I'm streaming high-level Protoss play," or whatever," and I would love a retweet from time to time." Because... you know what? Nine times out of ten that person's going to be like, "Hell yeah. We love having new streamers in our game."

Leigh "Maynarde" Mandalov

Rachel Rossin

Artist

*This conversation with
artist*
Rachel Rossin
was recorded 4/22/19

All images are from Man Mask, (2016) *by Rachel Rossin*

V95   Some readers of this book might know *Hot Shot,*
which is a shooter that uses a unique mechanic: time only
moves forward when the player moves. Your piece *Stalking
the Trace,* Which just opened in London uses a similar
mechanic.

RR   Yeah, it uses room-scale tracking in VR. So it's using the person's physical location to scrub time forward and backward. And it's funny because *Hot Shot* came out at the same time I started working on it—that's just the zeitgeist for you. But [*Stalking the Trace*] is quite different. I had to use some crazy hacks to get it to look right. I used Houdini to make these really gaudy, incredible, 'Christopher Nolan' explosions in VR. And then, depending on how your body moves in space these explosions, these disasters scrub forwards or backwards in time. Your body ends up feeling like this big lung that's controlling time. It took a long time to finish. Eventually, I knew it was done when I moved a giant fireball towards myself and actually felt warm. I tricked myself...

Rachel Rossin

V95   Do you find yourself using specific vocabulary to describe your work with VR to other people?

RR   That's a good question. I think of virtual reality as a kind of sentient installation. The best VR works, for me, are the works that have an awareness of the viewer, an awareness of the spectator. I'm all for passive VR experiences—I think that's also a distinct medium—but it's not the real reason [for VR], right? Sentient installations have an awareness of the viewer, and use viewers as "intermediaries," or "emissaries," or "interlopers."

V95   I'm curious to zoom in on your piece *Man Mask* which is described as "A guided meditation through land-

scapes taken from the game *Call of Duty: Black Ops*, drained of violence and transformed into an ethereal dream world."

RR   Yeah, that actually was a passive viewing experience. It was a challenge because it was commissioned by the New Museum, they wanted to distribute it for free, and I just didn't trust the app we had to use. So I challenged myself [to make a passive VR piece]. Embodiment, or body awareness, or meditation felt like a good place to start thinking about what a passive VR experience is.

I liked exploding these Call of Duty animation sequences, having them on a loop... When I was recording that piece—it was recorded in real-time—I was just randomly assigning the animation clips to the rigs and then

Rachel Rossin

messing around with shaders; and I liked that they were all collapsing in on each other in this sort of purgatory world. At the end of the piece you end up in this generic algorithm space, and there's this sort of GUI view of the what the bullet physics is doing, and then there's a pool, and all those oranges are falling...

V95   It's really beautiful. How'd you decide to work with *Call of Duty*, specifically?

RR   I was a big *Call of Duty* player, growing up. I loved first-person shooters for whatever reason—I'm admittedly just a video game addict. I can't start one or it'll take over my life. It's really been a problem as long as I've been alive and sentient. I used to mod games. And some of my work now is a similar kind of intervention. Or, a kind of statement on embodiment.

So I have a personal history with [*CoD*]. And back when I was able to start playing online I used a man's name and a boy's avatar. Anytime I had any representation online in any modding forums or anything I was using a "man mask," so that I could be a non-entity, or so that there was some democracy in the way I was treated.

V95   VR gaming is still a bit of a novelty. How do you feel VR is received in the art world?

RR   It's still cheesy. I mean, I feel like it's cheesy, and I make it. But it's absolutely a medium. I don't make predictions about where it's going or anything like that. I think that's just foolish. There will always be technology; there will always be tools with which to make work; and there will always ways of using those tools that tend towards novelty or spectacle. But I think experience should always be prioritized over spectacle or novelty.

And I think the medium [of VR] is also able to open up access [to art]. Some people don't like going to museums. Maybe it's nice that they can view a virtual reality work. I'm not saying one is better than the other. I just think it's interesting and it should exist.

In the beginning of *The Work of Art in the Age of Mechanical Reproduction* Walter Benjamin quotes Paul Valery who is describing the first time he heard a recorded symphony played back. It blew [Valery] away. He felt like he was in two places at once. The actual quote is much more poetic than how I'm putting it now [laughter], but, In some ways, that's my hope for VR. That it can be an experience that gives the feeling of being in the *presence* of something.